Emmons® Fashion Magic Jewelry

Cathryn S. Dippo and Janet L. Dippo

4880 Lower Valley Road, Atglen, PA 19310 USA

Dedication

For our parents who are no longer with us, G. Jack Dippo and Charles and Ida Speary. They will always be a part of us, and now, they are a part of this book.

"Emmons" and other associated trademarks are registered trademarks of the Emmons Jewelers, Inc. Their use herein is for identification purposes only. Emmons Jewelers, Inc. did not authorize this book nor furnish or approve of any of the information contained herein. The objects pictured in this book are from the collections of the authors of the book or various private collectors. This book is derived from the authors' independent research.

Copyright © 2005 by Cathryn S. Dippo and Janet L. Dippo
Library of Congress Control Number: 2005926941

All rights reserved. No part of this work may be reproduced or used in any form or by any means—graphic, electronic, or mechanical, including photocopying or information storage and retrieval systems—without written permission from the publisher.
The scanning, uploading and distribution of this book or any part thereof via the Internet or via any other means without the permission of the publisher is illegal and punishable by law. Please purchase only authorized editions and do not participate in or encourage the electronic piracy of copyrighted materials.
"Schiffer," "Schiffer Publishing Ltd. & Design," and the "Design of pen and ink well" are registered trademarks of Schiffer Publishing Ltd.

Designed by Mark David Bowyer
Type set in Zapf Calligraphy BT/Korinna BT

ISBN: 0-7643-2194-3
Printed in China
1 2 3 4

Published by Schiffer Publishing Ltd.
4880 Lower Valley Road
Atglen, PA 19310
Phone: (610) 593-1777; Fax: (610) 593-2002
E-mail: Info@schifferbooks.com

For the largest selection of fine reference books on this and related subjects, please visit our web site at
www.schifferbooks.com
We are always looking for people to write books on new and related subjects. If you have an idea for a book please contact us at the above address.

This book may be purchased from the publisher.
Include $3.95 for shipping.
Please try your bookstore first.
You may write for a free catalog.

In Europe, Schiffer books are distributed by
Bushwood Books
6 Marksbury Ave.
Kew Gardens
Surrey TW9 4JF England
Phone: 44 (0) 20 8392-8585; Fax: 44 (0) 20 8392-9876
E-mail: info@bushwoodbooks.co.uk
Free postage in the U.K., Europe; air mail at cost.

Contents

Preface 4
Acknowledgments 5
Overview and Book Organization 6
Introduction 7
    The Beginnings of Emmons Jewelry 7
    Selling Jewelry at Home Fashion Shows 9
    Boosting Sales Using Public Relations Campaigns 15
    The End of Emmons Jewelry 17
The Jewelry 19
    Emmons Jewelry Today 23
    Valuation 25
    Organizing a Collection 26
Clear Rhinestones, Crystal, and Aurora Borealis 27
Clear Rhinestones and Pearls 38
Pearls 41
Black and Shades of Grey 53
White 63
Blue and Turquoise 75
Green 86
Red, Pink, and Purple 93
Topaz, Citrine, Amber, Tortoiseshell, and Just Plain Brown 100
Yellow, Orange, and Coral 109
Multi-Colored and Miscellaneous 115
Just Silver 133
Silver and Gold 149
Just Gold 151
An Unsolved Mystery 174
Index 175

Preface

At some point, the collector reaches a point where just acquiring more objects for a collection is no longer sufficient. You learn that acquisition is enhanced by knowledge. Such knowledge can range from the basics, such as markings that aid in identification of objects, to the more complex, such as history related to the company that made them and the times in which they were made. Sometimes, your desire to know more about the how and why surpasses your need to acquire more.

What do you do when you reach this point? Write a book, of course. Writing a book gives you the pretext for contacting people and asking them all kinds of questions about things that happened twenty, thirty, forty, fifty years ago. Their stories provide more than just facts; they give the listener a sense of what it was like back then.

In this particular case, you get the feeling that these people truly enjoyed working for C. H. Stuart, Inc. Some were surprised and deeply hurt when the company filed for bankruptcy, discontinued the Emmons line, and laid them off—probably in that order of importance. Losing their jobs may have been traumatic at the time, but today they primarily express a sense of loss with respect to a wonderful place to work.

While the passage of time adds value to our collections, it also leads to a loss of data and knowledge. Several people we interviewed said that they had just recently thrown out boxes of stuff related to their work. Many of the people who could have provided details on certain aspects of company operations are no longer with us. This book is but a modest attempt to preserve some parts of the history of Emmons jewelry. We encourage those with materials related to any of the C. H. Stuart companies to donate them to the Arcadia Historical Society, 120 High Street, Newark, NY 14513, (315) 331-6409, arcadiahistory@novocon.net.

Acknowledgments

Finding information by and about a company that has been out of business for more than twenty years required help—lots of it. One of our first contacts was Chris Davis, Executive Director of the Arcadia Historical Society in Newark, New York. Always helpful, he suggested names of people to contact, searched for archival materials, and provided space for interviews. Staff at the Wayne County Clerk's Office, the Office of the County Historian, and the Surrogate's Court were very accommodating and went out of their way to be helpful.

Of course, the most helpful in terms of details about Emmons Jewelers, Inc., as a company, were its former employees. Bill Scheetz, who was its President during the 1960s, provided information about the start of the company and graciously invited Cathryn to his home to see some early pieces of jewelry. Tom Healy, former Vice President for Sales, patiently explained the structure and workings of the sales staff. Franklin Russell, who was the company's Associate Counsel, clarified issues related to copyrights and trademarks. Former editors of *Timely Topics* and *Manager's Weekly Bulletin* Dawn (Vande Viver) Levickas and Susan (Curtin) Wyner, respectively, provided copies of these house organs and insights into the day-to-day operations at company headquarters. Don Snow donated newsletters and other materials related to C. H. Stuart, Inc., and Gil Lewis, an employee in another Stuart subsidiary who became one of the first stockholders in Emmons, had miraculously kept all the annual reports to stockholders for the twenty years Emmons Jewelers existed as a separate business entity. By a stroke of luck, Patricia Meyer, a former designer for Royal Crest, returned from vacation and took the time to be interviewed before she even unpacked! Aileen Van Tyle, the first woman to become a Vice President at Sarah Coventry®, gave a vivid account of the first "test" parties. Camille Mongada, Field Vice President and winner of numerous awards including at least twenty-seven President's Trophies, was our source for a perspective from the field.

One of the hardest and most time consuming aspects of preparing a book like this is identifying the jewelry. In addition to materials provided by those mentioned above, copies of order forms from the 1950s were provided by Janet Robinson via her daughter Jan Venti, and later catalogs were provided by Deborah Robinson and Kay Oshel.

Special thanks to Nancy Schiffer, Donna Baker, Jeff Snyder, and others at Schiffer Publishing for providing advice and expertise without which this book would not have been possible, and to Janet's friends and colleagues Deborah Barnes, Nancy Getsi, and James Pearce who provided some much needed editorial advice.

Finally, but definitely not least, we thank our mother/mother-in-law Alice Louise Dippo and brother/husband Gordon Dippo. The former was probably the first to suggest we write this book. The latter was unquestionably the one who suffered the most during its preparation. Without their encouragement and support, it would never have happened.

Overview and Book Organization

The authors of this book are collectors. As collectors, our primary goal in preparing this book has been to create something a collector or would-be collector of Emmons jewelry would find useful for documenting and organizing their collection. To that end, we begin the book with information about the company responsible for Emmons jewelry—how it came into being, sold jewelry, established and maintained a sales force and, all too soon, ceased to exist.

Next, we turn to the jewelry. After providing general background material that will help in the identification and dating of the jewelry, we discuss various options for organizing a large collection. To date we have identified more than 1,300 different designs and 1,700 different pieces sold as Emmons jewelry, primarily between the mid-1960s and 1981. Thus, we believe the total number of designs probably approaches 2,000, and the number of different pieces could easily reach 3,000. Organizing and keeping track of a collection that could eventually reach such a size requires a plan.

We then present photographs of the jewelry organized as we physically organize our collections, which is basically by color. After carrying books around antique shows for our other collections that require continuous flipping from earrings to pins to rings to sets to determine if we have an item that is for sale, we have learned that one of the fastest ways to locate an item is by color. Although time is not the issue when sitting in front of the computer using online auctions, the location problem still exists. Using our method of color is not infallible, but it works much more often than not. This, of course, assumes one is willing to make notations on ownership in your book. We write all over ours.

Emmons jewelry is costume jewelry. With the exception of the Crown Collection and the 14 kt. jewelry introduced in the very last year or so of Emmons' existence, most of the jewelry is not real gold or silver nor are the stones real. While we have tried to be precise by using the words gold-tone or silver-tone and describing stones as imitation or plastic, there are instances where it just made more grammatical sense to leave out the qualifiers. Please do not assume an item is "real" if a qualifier is missing, rather assume that unless we specify the item is 14 kt. gold, 10 kt. gold-filled, cultured pearl, real jade, etc., it is not.

Introduction

"What is Fashion Magic? Fashion magic is combining your imagination with our jewelry! Fashion Magic is wearing one piece of jewelry many different ways! Fashion Magic is combining two pieces of jewelry to develop a whole new piece!"
—*Timely Topics*, August 1, 1975

Versatility, quality, and service were the watchwords of Emmons jewelry. It was sold only at home parties, where Fashion Show Directors demonstrated how to make Fashion Magic with Emmons jewelry, encouraging party participants to try on the jewelry and see for themselves its versatility. In selecting items for its line, the Jewelry Selection Committee focused on designs that exemplified the company's focus on versatility and quality. As a small, privately held company, Emmons Jewelers, Inc., set and enforced high standards of quality on its manufacturers. It believed in personalized service, from the invitation to attend a fashion show through the delivery of the jewelry. Each piece was fully guaranteed, and if you lost one earring, you could buy a replacement at reduced cost.

Incorporated in 1949, Emmons Jewelers, Inc., was the first company to use the party plan to sell costume jewelry in the United States. In its first twenty years, the company's best year was 1959, when it had over $5 million in net sales. In the 1970s, when various levels of the sales force competed against each other and against prior sales records during "Record Breaking Weeks," the top zone logged almost $600,000 in sales, and personal sales peaked at over $13,000 in 1980 for the three week period. Unfortunately, the parent company C. H. Stuart, Inc., overextended itself in the latter half of the decade and eventually filed for reorganization under Chapter 11 of the U. S. Bankruptcy Code in 1981. As part of the reorganization, sales of Emmons jewelry came to an end.

Today, Emmons jewelry is highly collectible. The high quality of design and manufacture so diligently pursued back then has resulted in timeless pieces of costume jewelry that are a pleasure to wear today.

The Beginnings of Emmons Jewelry

In 1864, Charles W. Stuart, a "manufacturing jeweler" in Syracuse, New York, decided to move west for health reasons and bought a farm on the north side of the village of Newark in the town of Arcadia, Wayne County, New York. With him were his wife, Caroline Emmons Stuart, his younger brother, John Electus, also a jeweler, and his mother, Adeline. Stuart's farm included several hundred fruit trees, and while Stuart was not interested in farming per se, he recognized the value of the trees on his property to others. So, he began to visit his

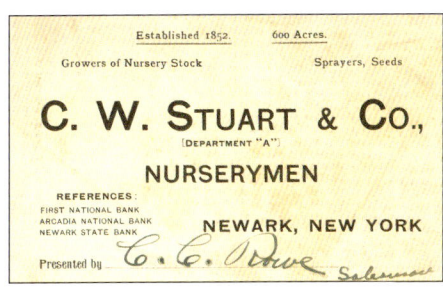

C. W. Stuart & Co., Nurserymen calling card.

neighbors for the purpose of peddling his trees. Slowly, he built up a business, hiring sales people and planting more trees, until he eventually formed a nursery company—C. W. Stuart & Company. Then, in 1895, he created a second company to compete with the first, followed by a third, a fourth, ... , until a total of thirteen nursery companies existed. One of these nursery companies was Emmons and Company, which had its incorporation papers filed on December 31, 1903.

Stuart companies produced a variety of products. From the House of Stuart, Glo-Gent Freshener, Sicilian Hand Cream, and Pure Spices Ground Nutmeg; from Stuart Distributors, Stuart's Bath Crystals; from Stuart Products, Stuart's Mentha-Rub Salve; and from Home Decorator's, Inc., a clear plastic coin bank.

C. W.'s son, Charles H. or Harry, graduated from Cornell University with a degree in chemistry and returned home to work in the nursery business. But his real interest was chemistry, so he set up a lab and created extracts—concentrated food flavorings. In 1908, C. H.

Stuart, Charles R. Clark, and James M. Pitkin incorporated J. M. Pitkin & Co. to manufacture and sell extracts, flavors, perfumes, and other chemical products using the same door-to-door direct-selling techniques the Stuarts had perfected in the nursery business. And following the successful model of the nursery business, additional chemical companies were created to compete against Pitkin, including one named Paul D. Newton & Co., Inc. Another of these companies was C. H. Stuart & Co., Inc., in 1924, with Lyman K. Stuart, Harry's son, as President. During the Depression, it became necessary to consolidate the many individual businesses into a few, but the philosophy of competition being good for business was not abandoned.

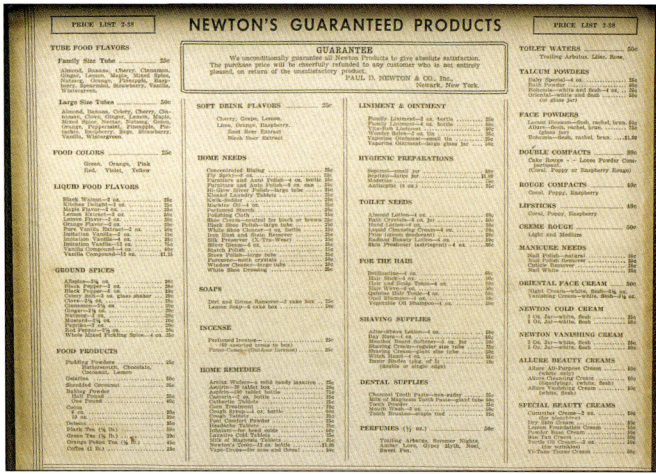

A price list pasted in the lid of a sample case for Newton's Guaranteed Products listing items such as food flavors, food colors, pudding, tea, coffee, stove polish, and personal care items ranging from cathartic tablets to face cream.

As business conditions stabilized, Lyman Stuart decided to expand in an entirely new direction—silver and flatware, since these items had been very popular as prizes and premiums. He did this by converting the product line of The Wayne Nurseries, Inc., and changing its name to Silver Service Club, Inc., in 1935. Once it was successful, additional companies were created, converted, or merged, and additional product lines in china and home furnishings were added. In every case, the new or converted company sold its products directly to its customers using door-to-door or home party methods.

Over the winter of 1948-49, difficulties in finding sufficient, good nursery stock led the management of C. H. Stuart & Co., Inc., (Lyman Stuart and others) to look for new product lines that might be pursued by the men running Emmons and Company. If the new company were successful, the Emmons and Company nursery business would be folded into one of the other nursery businesses. The board of directors decided on costume jewelry to be sold via home fashion shows, and Ed Farrell (then President of Emmons) and some of his staff, including Bill Scheetz, were given the task of figuring out how to do it.

Knowing nothing about jewelry, one of the first things the group did was hire a consultant, Irving Wolf, who had worked with Trifari. Wolf gathered together a collection of jewelry and brought it to Newark, where about 50 to 75 pieces were selected to be sold by Emmons Jewelers, Inc. With no experience in the home party business, the group also studied the business model of other home party firms, including Stanley Home Products, a particularly successful party plan business at the time.

To test the concept of selling costume jewelry at a home party, Aileen Van Tyle was asked to conduct a few test fashion shows. For the first one, someone simply went to Rochester, New York, and bought some jewelry for her to try to sell that evening at someone's home. According to Van Tyle, she had no script, and at one point she excused herself from the "party" to ask the men listening in another room if they had any suggestions about what to do next. She was simply told to keep doing what she had been doing. Learning from Van Tyle, Bill Scheetz held a party to see if men could do the job. Van Tyle's pioneer work demonstrated that it was possible to sell costume jewelry at a home fashion show.

The incorporation papers for Emmons Jewelers, Inc., were filed on April 21, 1949, listing Lyman K. Stuart, Paul D. Newton, Leslie J. Engleson, and E. C. Humeston as officers and subscribers. Egbert (Ed) F. Farrell, who had been President of Emmons and Company, became the first President.

A 1907 recipe booklet from Stuart's No-Al Food Flavors. Perhaps "No-Al" meant there was no alcohol in the flavorings.

Once the product had been selected and the means of selling designed, recruiting began in earnest. Classified ads were placed in newspapers to create a hiring pool from which men were interviewed, hired, and trained as area managers. These men then had to recruit, hire, and train others in their areas to be Fashion Show Directors. In the beginning, areas like Rochester, Syracuse, Buffalo, Cleveland, Indianapolis, and Chicago were targeted in one direction and Harrisburg, Philadelphia, etc. in another.

The first year, the company ran a deficit of $827, but in the second year (fiscal year 1951), the company had a net income of $173,606 and paid its first dividend. Declaring the business a success, C. W. Stuart and Co. changed the name of the old nursery business Emmons and Company to Sarah Coventry, Inc., increased its capital stock and converted it into a rival jewelry company with Lyman Stuart's eldest son C. W. "Bill" Stuart as president. (Lyman Stuart's daughter had a child named Sarah Coventry Beale; thus, the two Stuart jewelry companies were named after Lyman Stuart's grandmother and granddaughter.) Sarah Coventry had its own staff both at headquarters and in the field, and ran its business independently of Emmons. The race was on.

Selling Jewelry at Home Fashion Shows

Fashion Show Directors had two tasks: recruiting and selling. Recruiting was by far the most important, since they had to recruit both hostesses and potential new Fashion Show Directors. Hostesses were responsible for inviting guests, providing display space, and then, after the show, collecting money and distributing the purchased jewelry. At the party, the Fashion Show Director (FSD) laid a cloth over two card tables (or equivalent) to create a display background and began the fashion show. In the early years, the jewelry was rolled in aqua flannel and carried in a brown faux-alligator satchel-type briefcase; later on it was rolled in lightweight foam and carried in a large gold valise. As the roll was unwound and an item revealed, the FSD lifted it off the roll and talked about it—what style and colors of clothing it would accent, on what types of occasions it might be the perfect eye catcher or gift, and so forth. The FSD engaged the guests by demonstrating how it would look on them and how it could be worn in various ways by adding another piece or changing how it was worn. Once all the items had been revealed and laid out on the display table, the guests were invited and encouraged to handle the items, try them on, and have their friends admire the results.

During the try-on period, the FSD began the most important aspect of her job—recruiting potential new Fashion Show Directors. She talked to each guest individually, promoting the advantages of becoming an FSD. For the company to grow and increase its sales, it needed more sales staff. For an FSD to be really successful, she needed to move up the management ladder so that she could earn commissions on what the FSDs working for her sold. The jewelry sold itself; the company did not. The company needed convincing spokespersons who ardently believed in the Emmons way.

Turnover was high. For example, the fiscal year 1955 stockholders' report states:

> We started the year with 1,285 salespeople, but all during the summer we lost them faster than we could recruit new ones. ... [net] loss of 385 ... despite the fact we recruited a total of 1,006 new salespeople.

The entire system was based on incentives. Hostesses earned free jewelry if their guests bought more than so many dollars-worth of jewelry. Fashion Show Directors earned commissions on sales and special prizes if their sales exceeded some amount or one of the guests at their parties became an FSD. One special prize was a cashmere and mink sweater by Faviani and Annis. To get the sweater for free, one had to earn 2000 Magic Mirror credits, i.e., one credit for each $1 in net sales and 100 credits for each qualified recruit, all during the period November 5, 1960, to January 6, 1961. Earlier, in the mid-1950s, prizes included silver tea sets and sets of stainless steel flatware, items still cherished by former FSDs like Janet Robinson. An unusual prize from the 1950s was a set of two aluminum porch chairs for one recruit!

As with most home sales programs, Emmons thanked its hostesses by allowing them to earn gifts. In the mid-1960s hostesses earned an allowance of $1 for every guest who placed an order; $1 for every Showcase (catalog) order; $3 extra for having a show within a week or two of the show she attended; and $1 for one book-

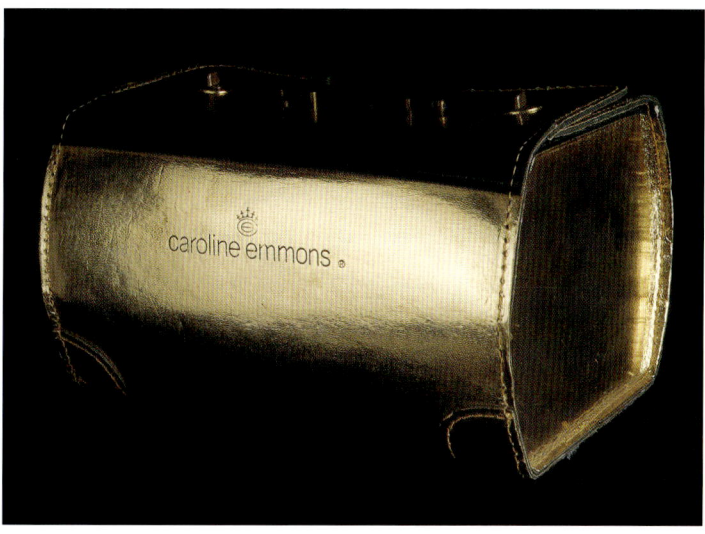

Gold valise used by Fashion Show Directors.

ing, $4 for two bookings, or $7 for three or more bookings obtained at, and to be held within thirty days of, her show. If sales totaled $100 net and two bookings were made at the show, the hostess was eligible for a Queen Hostess Gift. In 1965, three Queen Hostess Gifts were offered: **Symphonie** (see p. 53), **Fashion Flair** (see p. 151), and **Queen of Fashion** (see p. 38). Through 1971, the hostess plan remained basically the same, although the amounts and jewelry selections changed.

The Queen of Fashion listing from the 1965 *Showcase*.

The hostess plan was simplified in 1972 when the "2 & 3 $AVINGS PLAN" was introduced and ensemble pricing eliminated. Moreover, the plan was promoted as helping hostesses win, as opposed to earn, Royal Hostess Gifts. (Under the savings plan, guests could buy two items at regular price and get the third at a savings of 50 percent or more.) Hostesses whose shows earned over $100 with two or more bookings chose from six Royal Hostess Gifts: **Royal Princess** (bracelet and earrings), **Coin of the Realm** (disc belt), **Daughter of the Nile** (necklace and bracelet), **Legacy** (bracelet and earrings, see p.120), **Roman Holiday** (fill-in necklace, see. p. 83), and **Sorcery** (lavalliere pin, see p. 47). Over the next few years, qualifications for the Royal Hostess prizes were eventually raised to $150 in sales and three bookings. (In 1975, the savings plan became the "2 & 4" Plan. With the purchase of any two items, a third could be purchased for $4.00.) While the Hostess Plan continued in 1976, it no longer offered any special pieces of jewelry. Then, in 1981, the Royal Hostess gifts were back; however, they were not nearly as bold or imaginative as in earlier years, and the qualifiers were steeper. A $300 show with two bookings yielded the hostess **Diamond Girl** (see p. 22), "a genuine 1 pt. diamond in a bright cut sterling silver setting…carried on a goldentone wire heart motif." The hostess had a choice of **My Fair Lady** ("a vermeil finish sterling silver bow floats on a…14 kt. gold filled cable chain") or **Juliette** ("…Black onyx, blue onyx, jade, red onyx, and tiger eye are gracefully spaced on a 15"-17" adjustable curb chain") for a $200 show and two bookings.

By the 1970s, promotions and competitions for the sales staff proliferated. Every month there was at least one special promotion going on to provide a new incentive for the sales staff and another for hostesses or buyers.

A *Showcase* page from 1976 explaining the Boutique Savings Plan.

For example, in 1975 the year began with the annual Caroline Awards Campaign (December 30-March 30), which was followed by the Convention '75 competition (April 14-June 8). June 9-22 were "Think Pink" weeks (win a pink attaché case with $300 net personal sales), July 7-August 31 the "Summer Wishes" contest, September 8-November 2 the "Gold Rush Days" fall recruiting push, November 3-23 "Record Breaking Weeks," and November 3-December 28 "New You" recruiting (earn a hair dryer or styling wand for just one qualified recruit). Specials included Hostess Half Price Weeks (December 30-February 2 and July 21-August 17), a Zodiac pendant special (April 28-May 25), Caroline's "BBB" Hostess Special (June 23-July 6), Caroline's Summer Customer Sale (June 23-July 13), a ring and pierced earring hostess special (August 18-September 14), and a special Christmas Gift Savings offer.

To keep the sales staff motivated, weekly assemblies were held, and weekly newsletters were distributed to both management (*Weekly Assembly Guide*) and FSDs (*Timely Topics*). The weekly assembly was part staff meeting and part pep rally. The *Guide* provided a series of questions or topics to be used in the training portion of the meeting. Slogans abounded: C.O.M.E. (Caroline's Opportunity Meeting for Everyone), "Say Yes, I'm Yours," "I can, You can, We can," "Try Caroline and Believe." Sometimes games were used to engage the salespeople through competition. For example, in the summer of 1975, the winners of a "Fashion Match-It" board game were to be given the opportunity to submit an original idea to the jewelry designers in Providence. Attendees (FSDs, Fashion Leaders, and Unit Managers) were expected to provide at least three leads or names of people who had expressed some interest in becoming an FSD—each week.

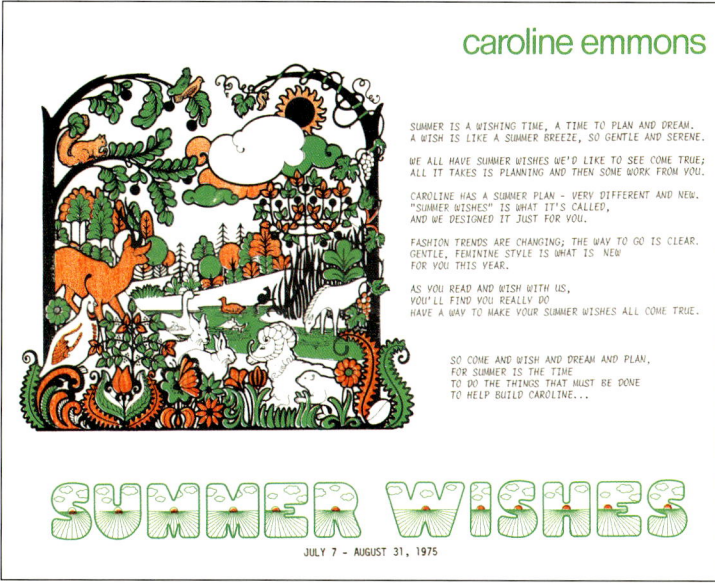

A pair of motivational flyers distributed at weekly sales assemblies describing incentives to boost sales.

The 1975 promotional "Summer Wishes" generated another motivational tool, the "Fashion Match-It" board game.

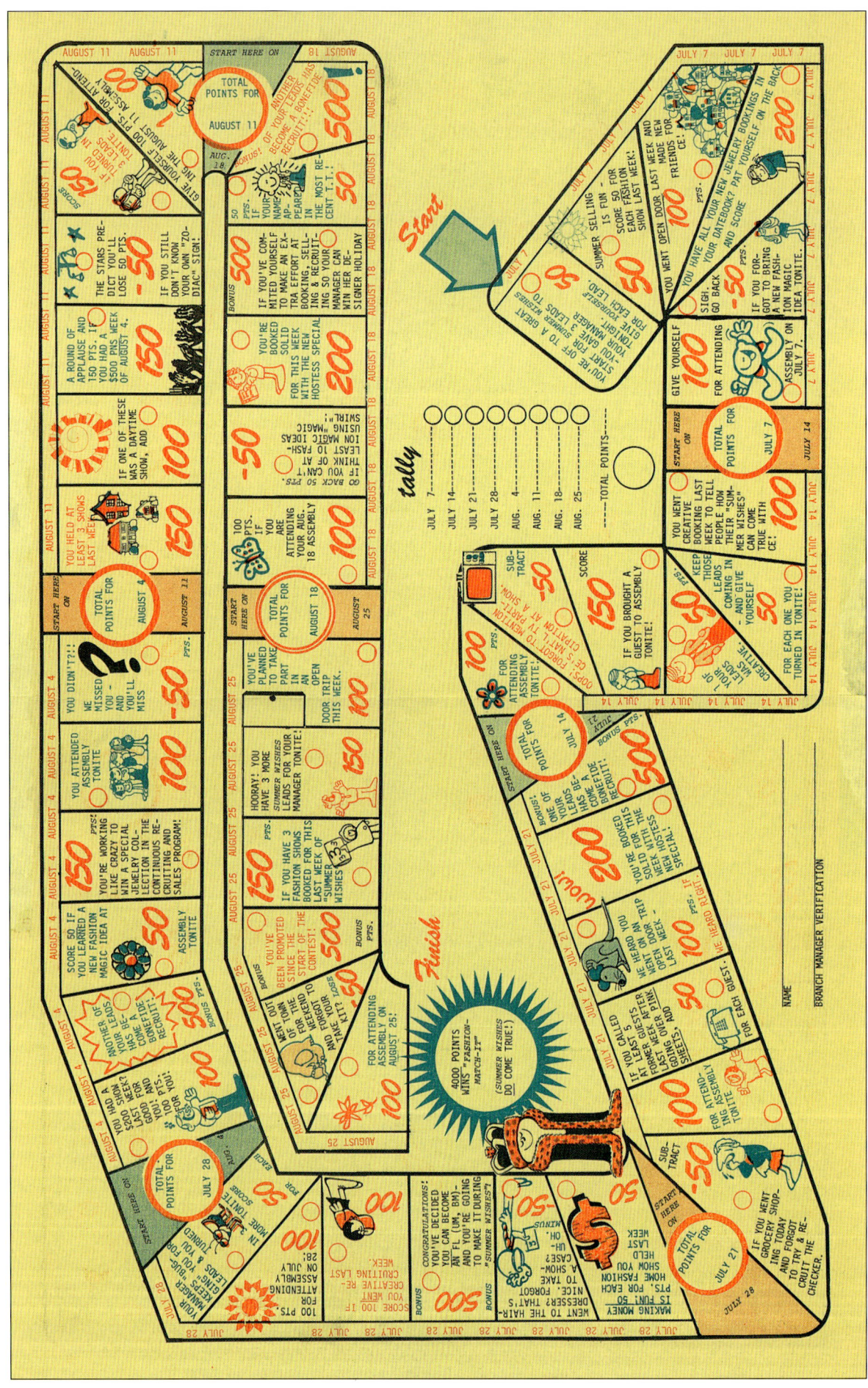

The "Fashion Match-It" board game.

The April 11, 1975, issue of Timely Topics provides an excellent illustration of what Fashion Magic jewelry was all about.

which began in 1966, was awarded quarterly to the top area, region, branch, and unit in sales. The Vice President's Trophy, initiated in 1974, was awarded quarterly to the top branch and unit recruiting teams.

A collection of company service and convention meeting pins. All except the Stuart 20-year pin are *courtesy of Dawn Levickas*.

One early recruiting award was a reproduction of a pin purportedly designed by Charles W. Stuart for his bride Caroline Emmons. On the occasion of the dedication of the new C. H. Stuart, Inc., headquarters on May 15, 1977, the same design was incorporated into a locket pendant that was distributed only to the guests at the dedication.

Timely Topics provided the proverbial "pat on the back" recognition for the far flung field force. Photographs abounded, showing FSDs and managers receiving awards, acknowledging promotions, and attending conventions. Salespeople had to earn the right to attend conventions through sales or recruiting. The home office staff also received recognition, so that the field staff could associate faces with the names of the people who provided them with various services. Salespeople were encouraged to submit suggestions for how to make Fashion Magic with pieces of Emmons jewelry for inclusion in Timely Topics. One such suggestion told how to show **Boutique Three** twelve different ways and another described thirty-five different ways to wear **Spellbinder** (see p. 59).

By the 1970s, Emmons had a very extensive awards program that included an Honor Key Program, Hall of Fame, and the President's and Vice President's Trophies. To be inducted into the Hall of Fame, one had to have 60 personal recruits; to earn the Triple Diamond Hall of Fame required 130 recruits. The President's Trophy,

This locket (marked Caroline Awards 1977) and pin (marked Caroline Emmons, Newark, N.Y.) are reproductions of a design purportedly done by C. W. Stuart for his bride, Caroline Emmons.

Competition was a key motivator. By the 1970s, the art of engendering competition among the sales force had evolved into two major competitions—Record Breaking Weeks and the Caroline Awards. Record Breaking Weeks (two or three weeks in early November) were a push to generate Christmas sales. In this way, direct-selling did not differ from in-store merchandising; good Christmas sales were vital to the bottom line. At the end of the Record Breaking Weeks, company headquarters held a telethon with each unit calling in to report its total sales and who in the unit had the highest personal sales. One name stands out from all the rest: Norma Miles. She had the highest personal sales of a Unit Manager in 1975, 1976, 1977, and 1978, then as a Fashion Leader in 1979 and as a Branch Manager in 1980. She logged $13,471.37 in personal sales during Record Breaking Weeks 1980.

contest period became Princess Caroline. (After a couple of years, the top Branch Manager rather than Unit Manager earned the honor.) At the three-day awards ceremony, which was held in such places as the Bahamas (1972), Hawaii (1973), San Juan (1974), Las Vegas (1975), and Miami Beach (1976), Princess Caroline reigned. From the time she walked off the airplane to be greeted with flowers and a limousine ride to the hotel until she received her crown and robes at the awards banquet, she was treated like royalty.

The red apple charm bracelet was a promotional item and not available for sale. *Courtesy of Dawn Levickas.*

A charm bracelet with a collection of charms commemorating awards ceremonies at various convention locations and sales promotions. On the **Wavelength** bracelet, clockwise from the clasp are: stylized USA flag from the 1979 convention in Washington, D.C.; banjo from the 1978 convention in Nashville; riverboat from the 1978 Caroline Awards in New Orleans; palm trees on an enameled background from the 1980 convention in Florida; 1980 convention (reverse of 7 Springs); home office dedication ceremonies, August 6, 1977, Newark, N.Y.; orchid on green background from the 1977 Caroline Awards in Hawaii; "I can, You can, We can" from Caroline Awards in Miami; gold record from R.B.W. (Record Breaking Weeks promotion); peach blossom from 1975 convention in Atlanta; Queen of Hearts from 1979 Caroline Awards in Las Vegas; 7 Springs in enamelwork from the 1980 convention. *Courtesy of Dawn Levickas.*

The Caroline Awards focused on recruiting during the first quarter of the year. Since recruiting was primarily a management responsibility (FSDs gave the names of potential recruits to their managers, who did the interviewing and hiring), the top Unit Manager during the

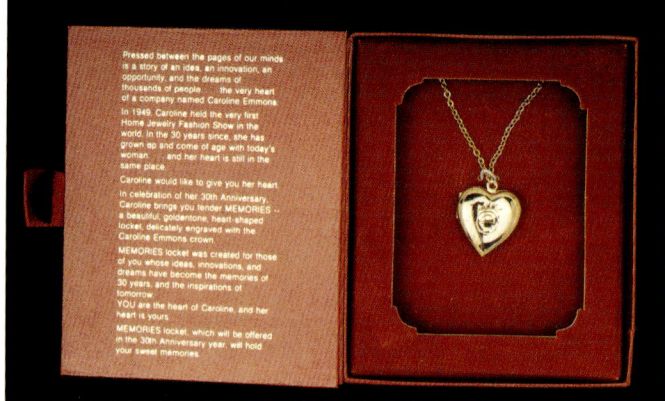

Memories. A locket issued in honor of Caroline's 30th Anniversary. Text on the box reads, "Pressed between the pages of our minds is a story of an idea, an innovation, an opportunity, and the dreams of thousands of people…the very heart of a company named Caroline Emmons. In 1949, Caroline held the very first home Jewelry Fashion Show in the world. In the 30 years since, she has grown up and come of age with today's woman…and her heart is still in the same place. Caroline would like to give you her heart in celebration of her 30th Anniversary. Caroline brings you tender MEMORIES—a beautiful, goldentone, heart-shaped locket, delicately engraved with the Caroline Emmons crown. MEMORIES locket was created for those of you whose ideas, innovations, and dreams have become the memories of 30 years, and the inspirations of tomorrow. YOU are the heart of Caroline, and her heart is yours. MEMORIES locket, which will be offered in the 30th Anniversary year will hold you sweet memories." *Courtesy of Dawn Levickas.*

Boosting Sales Using Public Relations Campaigns

March, June, September, and November 1953; March, June, and September 1954; and in *Harper's Bazaar* in September 1957.

This Emmons ad appeared in *Harpers Bazaar*, January 1953, 35.

A unique display of Emmons jewelry is shown in this ad from *Vogue*, September 15, 1959, 30.

A re-creation of the combination of the **Sparklets** pin fastened on the **Palisades** bracelet as shown in the *Harpers Bazaar* ad.

Recruiting was the primary focus of early advertising. In the 1950s, the company was very conservative with its advertising budget. One full-page advertisement appeared in the January 1953 issue of *Harper's Bazaar*; another in the September 1959 issue of *Vogue*. The 1962 stockholders' report noted that a national advertisement was being planned for that year, the first since 1959. In comparison, Sarah Coventry placed ads in *Vogue* in

Sometime around 1960, the company began using the public relations consulting firm of Ruder & Finn. For at least five years, Emmons received a Public Relations Award from the National Association of Direct Selling Companies, even though it did not make a major investment in advertising. In 1963, their award-winning entry stated that their entire public relations costs were less than a two-page advertisement in *Life* magazine.

One important facet of the public relations campaign involved having celebrities photographed wearing Emmons jewelry. These celebrity photographs were published in a booklet entitled *Celebrity of the Week*, which was distributed to all salespeople to aid them in recruiting. None of the celebrities were paid; they participated for the opportunity to gain exposure to the thousands of women who attended Emmons fashion shows. Emmons also sponsored *R.S.V.P.*, a half-hour radio program. During the program, commentator Graham Scott interviewed a guest star, who was given the opportunity to select pieces of Emmons jewelry. Included among the stars interviewed were Jane Fonda, Kim Hunter, Patricia Barry, Burl Ives, Viveca Lindfors, and Woody Herman.

A pair of multi-functional cardboard tags issued for use in recruiting new sales people.

The *1976 Spring and Summer Showcase* featuring Tawny Godin, Miss America 1976.

Also, beginning in 1960, Emmons provided the winner of the Miss New York State contest an opportunity to select an Emmons fashion jewelry wardrobe. The winner (along with her chaperone) was invited to visit Emmons headquarters in Newark to select the wardrobe. Most seem to have selected everything. In 1976, Tawny Godin, Miss New York State 1975, was selected Miss America. On her victory walk down the runway in Atlantic City, she wore **Crystal Lights**. Her picture was featured on the covers of the two 1976 Emmons *Showcases*, the only instances when a celebrity graced the catalog covers. Miss America also had the opportunity to select a jewelry wardrobe, but in this case, Emmons staff went to New York to meet with her.

Emmons jewelry could also be seen in the movies, on Broadway, and on television. Lee Remick and Eve Arden wore Emmons jewelry in *Anatomy of a Murder*. Stars in the Broadway plays *Sleeping Prince*, *Enter Laughing*, and others wore Emmons jewelry. More than twenty-five Emmons FSDs appeared as contestants on various game shows in 1963 alone—wearing Emmons jewelry, of course!

By the 1970s, television was heavily used in the company's public relations campaigns. Emmons jewelry could be seen on daytime shows such as *$10,000 Pyramid*, *Split Second*, *Magnificent Marble Machine*, and *Money Maze*.

In 1975, a major new public relations campaign was launched called "Little Girl Next Door." Promotional materials began with "Caroline Emmons is not the little girl next door" and went on to say what Caroline Emmons *is*—"an Unlimited Opportunity," "a new corporate headquarters building," "Tawny Godin, Miss America (1976)," "jewelry 'fit' for a queen," "a Career with UNLIMITED potential," and "people, fashion fun," for example.

The "Little Girl Next Door" as she appeared on the cover of *Timely Topics*, August 29, 1975.

The End of Emmons Jewelry

With the emphasis on public relations in the early to mid-1960s, the addition of the Crown Collection in 1964, and a new sales promotion manager in 1966, Emmons increased its sales by 32 percent in 1966 over the prior year. The company even took the first steps towards going international, submitting an application for doing business in Japan. However, Emmons was by now the little sister of Sarah Coventry.

In 1967, Emmons reported only modest gains while Sarah Coventry reported a 25 percent increase in sales, primarily in its foreign operations (Canada, United Kingdom, and Australia). In a 1968 interview with the local newspaper, the president of Sarah Coventry, Inc., Rex Wood, predicted $50 million in sales in 1968; Emmons had barely more than $2 million in net sales for the same year. Sarah Coventry did not just all of a sudden take off in comparison to Emmons. At the end of its first five years, Sarah Coventry's sales were $4 million and at the end of ten years $25 million.

In 1969, Emmons Jewelers, Inc., and the remaining silver and home decorating companies were merged into C. H. Stuart & Co., Inc., which by now had expanded to include eight manufacturing divisions, nine sales divisions, nursery operations, warehouse and shipping facilities, and test market services. The next year Emmons celebrated its 21st birthday and "marked its coming of age" with a new name—Caroline Emmons—and a new public relations consultant, Mathison Advertising of Rochester, New York.

Sarah Coventry, Inc., was merged into C. H. Stuart, Inc., (the name was changed in 1974) in 1977, the year in which C. H. Stuart, Inc., dedicated its new showcase headquarters, called Stuart Park, on the southern outskirts of Newark village. Construction had begun on the 125,000-square-foot facility in 1975. Each division had its own space, including lounge area, pantry or kitchenette, custodian supply room, and restrooms. Personnel were strongly discouraged from fraternizing with the competition.

At the time of the dedication, a bronzed medal was issued commemorating 125 years of achievement (1852-1977). It was inscribed with the following words: "The dreams and visions which find their culmination here are not the product of any one individual. Rather, they reflect the imagination and effort of thousands of employees, representatives, customers, and associates. It is to them that this building is dedicated."

1979 was a year of many changes within C. H. Stuart, Inc. Several divisions were shut down: Gateway (a home decorating company started in 1974), Sarah Coventry of Australia, and Sarah Coventry operations in the United Kingdom. As a result of the closings, some staff were moved around. The managing director of Sarah Coventry Australia became president of Caroline Emmons, and several senior Gateway managers were also moved into Caroline Emmons. In addition, C. H. Stuart, Inc., incorporated in the state of Delaware.

The inside covers of the booklet given out at the headquarters dedication ceremony show the major divisions of C. H. Stuart, Inc.

The cover of the booklet from the headquarters dedication ceremony shows an artist's rendering of the new building.

Abruptly, in January 1981, C. H. Stuart, Inc., laid off 150 employees and cut the salaries of its 165 management and supervisory personnel by 10 percent. Its president and executive vice president resigned. On March 6, 1981, C. H. Stuart, Inc., filed for reorganization under Chapter 11 in the U.S. Bankruptcy Court in Rochester. The company had lost $24 million over the previous three years and had 1,700 creditors. It blamed increased operating costs, over expansion, and loss of sales staff to competitors.

When the company began its reorganization, it had twelve product divisions. The reorganization plan called for consolidating everything except Artcraft Concepts under the Sarah Coventry name. The company was to be run by executives of Catamore Company of Rhode Island, which had supplied much of Sarah Coventry's jewelry and was therefore a major creditor, with financial backing from Bennett S. Lebow. Sarah Coventry Canada and the Liege jewelry manufacturing plant in New Hampshire were to be sold.

The Caroline Emmons division was merged with Sarah Coventry. In August 1981, Sarah Coventry ran a classified ad for one day in thirty-five cities to recruit additional salespeople. It currently had 3,500. Potential salespeople would have to buy a sales kit that ranged in price from $220 ($547 retail) for the costume jewelry kit to $2,500 ($7,000 retail) for a kit containing 14 kt. gold and diamond jewelry. Individual items would sell for $7 to $3,000 (the latter for a wristwatch with a 24 kt. gold ingot face).

In January 1982, C. H. Stuart, Inc., officially became Sarah Coventry, Inc.

The Jewelry

"You can measure the difference in our fashion-minded jewelry ... versatile for today's woman with an eye for tomorrow ... something for every mood and mode ... fully guaranteed and reasonably priced."
—Caroline Emmons recruiting brochure, c. 1980

More than twenty years have passed since the last piece of Caroline Emmons jewelry was sold at a home fashion show. While the small company that sold it may have struggled for over thirty years to recruit and maintain a sufficient sales force to make the business profitable, it never really had to worry about selling the jewelry. The high quality of its design and manufacture, along with reasonable prices, insured that those who saw the jewelry at a fashion show bought it.

Emmons prided itself on providing "fine products, good service, and reasonable prices." Quality was not just a matter of words. Susan Wyner, editor of *Manager's Weekly Bulletin* in the mid-1970s, talked of wearing **Jet Elegance** for weeks, including in the shower, to test how well it would hold-up over time and in extreme conditions.

The first line of jewelry consisted of 50 to 75 pieces. Twice a year, some new pieces were added to the collection and some old ones dropped. In 1964, Emmons listed 44 earrings, 31 pins, 20 necklaces and chokers, 8 bracelets, 8 rings, 16 men's jewelry items, 7 pieces of junior jewelry, a sweater guard, necklace and bracelet extensions, **Wonder Clips**, and a ring box for a total of 139 different items with 84 different names. In the very last catalog, for spring 1981, there were several hundred items but only around 125 different names, since there were many chains of various lengths in both gold- and silver-tone and earrings in both clip and pierced versions.

Festival. The large white earrings are Emmons from 1972. The pin and earrings on the right are from Sarah Coventry in 1975. Emmons used the name again in 1975 for a necklace with colored rods (not shown).

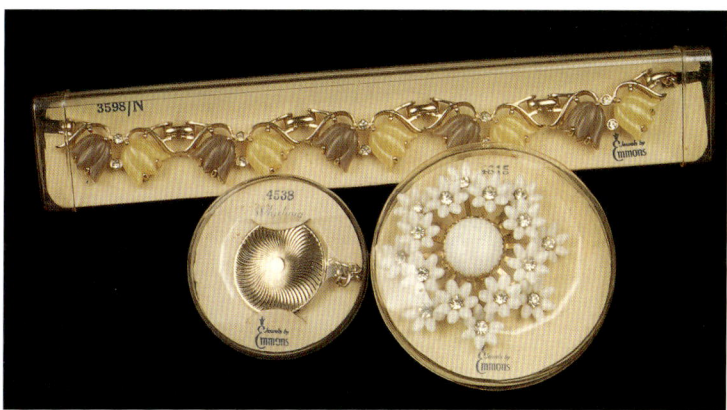

The jewelry came in clear plastic containers from the 1950s through the early 1960s.

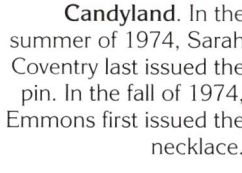

Candyland. In the summer of 1974, Sarah Coventry last issued the pin. In the fall of 1974, Emmons first issued the necklace.

From the beginning each design was given a name. The right name helped an item sell better. Some names were considered so successful they were used over and over again with a new design after the older design was discontinued. Examples include **Americana**, **Caprice**, **Mystique**, **Roman Holiday**, **Sonnet**, and **Victorian**. Inspiration for some names may have come from other companies or vice versa. Examples of items from both Emmons and Sarah Coventry with the same names were **Candyland** and **Festival**. Early packaging, which consisted of clear plastic tubes and round boxes with removable lids, did not include an item's name, only its item number.

Sometime around 1960, Emmons began printing catalogs that it called *Showcases*. Prior to that time, FSDs received no formal written documentation about the jewelry. Many created their own index card files. Quite to the contrary, FSDs for Sarah Coventry were given what was called a cardex file, which in the early days contained mimeographed pieces of paper containing mostly text with an occasional drawing (no photographs).

The early catalogs were similar to the cardex files in that they contained a flowery description of the item, along with a picture. By 1970 the descriptions had disappeared and more artistic photographs were used to display the jewelry.

A 1965 *Showcase* page illustrating a flowery jewelry description, this one for **Rainbow Star**.

Emmons never manufactured any of the jewelry it sold. In the beginning, all of its jewelry was purchased from manufacturers in the Providence, Rhode Island, area. Two of the early manufacturers used were Bergère and C. Ray Randall. In later years, Lang and Catamore were important suppliers. Salesmen for the various manufacturers visited Newark to display their wares to the Jewelry Selection Committee. For Emmons to consider marketing an item, the manufacturer had to give Emmons exclusive rights to the item in order to insure that the item would not be sold in retail stores.

The trend for more artistic photos of the jewelry rather than lengthy descriptions can be seen in this page from a 1976 *Showcase*.

Exclusive rights to a particular design did not mean that similar designs were not purveyed to other distributors. Designers often developed a general design and then modified it to create a number of specific designs that used the same components or manufacturing process. Thus, Emmons and Sarah Coventry often had quite similar designs for sale.

Similar designs appeared in both the Emmons (left, **Gold Lace**) and Sarah Coventry (right, **Fanfare**) collections.

Beginning in 1961, some items were manufactured in Newark. As the Stuart's jewelry manufacturing firm of Royal Crest grew, more items were made locally. However, Royal Crest could never have produced all the jewelry needed by Emmons and Sarah Coventry. In fact, it was not until C. H. Stuart, Inc., created Liege manufacturing in New Hampshire in the late 1970s that it had the capability of producing cast jewelry. Royal Crest did not make jewelry parts, but rather assembled parts made elsewhere and plated the final product. The rhinestones they used were made by Swarovski; the semi-precious stones came from Asia or Germany; the glass stones from Germany; and the plastic stones from the U.S., Germany, and some Asian countries.

Royal Crest was generally treated like the other suppliers; its designs competed with those of the other manufacturers. However, there were times when Emmons (and Sarah Coventry) requested Royal Crest to create something specific. One such case was the Emmons' **Mother's Pin**, which was designed by Patricia Meyer.

Over the years, several special collections were added by Emmons. The first was the Crown Collection of semi-precious stone jewelry that was introduced in the fall of 1964. The initial Crown Collection consisted of **Sprig of**

Jade (a spray pin with Wyoming jade and cultured pearl and leaf-motif earrings with a nestled cultured pearl, see p. 43), **Jeweled Charm** (a gold-filled bracelet chain and charm with a cultured pearl surrounded by semi-precious stones of Wyoming jade, adventurine, sodolite, and rose quartz, see p. 130), **Amber Royal** (a genuine amber stone on twelve karat gold-filled pendant chain, see p. 107), **Sterling Faith** (a sterling bracelet chain with a hand-engraved cross on a sterling charm), and **Elegance Engraved** (cuff links and tie bar—or tie tac—with a hand-engraved star-fire design).

Not until ten years later, in the Fall of 1974, was another special collection added to the line—the Boutique Collection. Described as "high fashion, high style, and exclusive jewelry designs … for women everywhere who want something special … ," items in the collection were more expensive and, thus, while they could be used as a regular price purchase toward the 2 & 4 Plan, they could not be purchased for $4. In fact, however, only two of the five items in the collection were new items—**Fifth Avenue** and **Roman Holiday**, and the three carry-over designs—**Spellbinder**, **Fashion Bangles**, and **Boutique Three**—had been excluded from the 2 & 3 Plan. (The 2 & 3 Plan changed to the 2 & 4 Plan between Spring 1974 and Fall 1974.) Moreover, the price for **Boutique Three** jumped 38 percent and that for **Spellbinder** 25 percent. Thus, the addition of this special collection appears to have been more of a response to rising costs than a change in customer tastes.

A 1978 *Showcase* page showing the **Mother's Pin** designed especially for Emmons.

On the other hand, the addition of the 14 kt. gold-filled Midas Collection in late 1979 clearly was in response to customer demand. It was touted as being "tailored to blend with casual fashions to attract attention by day and with dramatic dress-ups to capture those bright lights by night." Then, in 1980 a necklace and bracelet in 14 kt. plumb gold were added. These items came in brown and gold boxes.

Examples of packaging from late 1979 for the "Midas Collection." Box on right contains **Diamond Girl**. *Courtesy of Dawn Levickas.*

Emmons also had pieces of jewelry designed for special occasions. Two documented instances were the 1964 New York World's Fair and the 1980 Winter Olympics. For the New York World's Fair, a pin was designed to be given to the wives of the presidents of electric light and power companies and other distinguished visitors to the Tower of Light. The 1980 Winter Olympics pendant and pin consisted of a pair of skis with a set of crossed poles.

Emmons took pride in the quality of their designs. In 1969, it won the Swarovski Award for excellence in design (see *Showcase* photo on p. 20).

A very unusual and delicate piece, this light bulb pin was designed for a world's fair. Made entirely in gold tone, the 1" x .75" bulb is painted a silvery white.

Jet Elegance and **Golden Elegance** were long-running favorites in the Boutique Collection.

Emmons Jewelry Today

Identification of Emmons jewelry can be problematic for the collector today. Emmons did not request copyright protection for any of its designs until 1959. Even then, not all designs or items of the same design were submitted for copyright. By 1969, when Emmons merged into C. H. Stuart & Co., Inc., which filed to have Emmons Jewelers, Inc.'s, copyrights transferred to them, there were only about 275 copyright-registered items.

The copyright symbol is clearly visible on the back of the carved coral bracelet.

Jewelry came on cards showing the number assigned to the item.

Because Emmons did not begin copyrighting its jewelry until 1959, items sold before then will not contain the copyright mark. The items in the 1953 *Harper's Bazaar* ad that we have found are not marked, nor are boxed items. Thus, we believe that most items from the early 1950s will not be marked at all. On the other hand, the items shown in the 1959 *Vogue* ad are marked "EmJ," and most of the items copyrighted through April 1960 are recorded as being marked "EmJ" in the copyright card catalog.

Some unmarked pieces may be identified, at least tentatively as Emmons, via other markings. For example, the engraving on the clip back earring shown below is similar to that of the left-most one in the photograph of the three earring backs, except that it does not contain the "EmJ" mark. Similarly, the design on the pin shown on p. 168 is the same as that on the back of the earrings shown on p. 48.

The mark on this earring back is a variation of another mark.

Here are several examples of marks used on the backs of earrings.

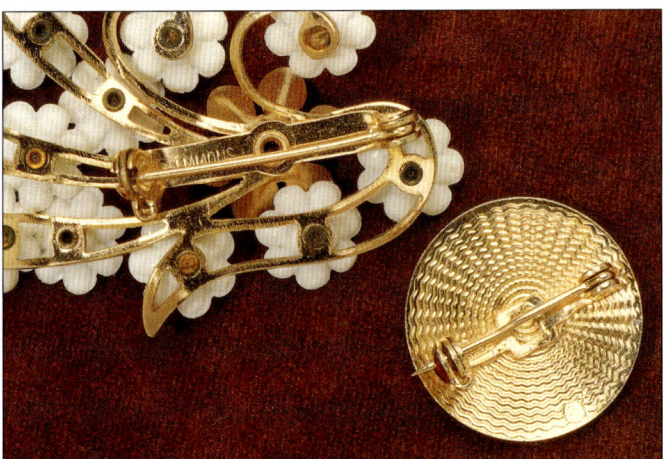

On the left, a pin is marked Emmons but without a copyright symbol. The pin on the right is unmarked.

The backs of the earrings above (front side shown on p. 48) are the same as the front of the pin.

Besides starting to copyright its jewelry, Emmons also began putting unique "tags" on necklaces or chokers with fish hook fasteners—a script letter *E* with a crown over it. Later, necklaces with spring-ring closures were marked with a rectangular hang tag containing the copyright symbol and the word "Emmons." After the company changed its name to Caroline Emmons in 1970, a round hang tag containing the word "Emmons" on one side and a logo consisting of a *c* surrounding an *e* and capped with a gold crown were used.

A variety of hang tags used to mark Emmons bracelets and necklaces.

Despite the uniqueness of the original gold crown tag, it was never trademarked. In fact, the first trademark filing was not made until 1956, when the word Emmons was registered, claiming first use on March 25, 1949. Subsequently, the company trademarked the word marks Fashion Magic, Caroline Emmons, Caroline, and Lady Caroline, all for jewelry, claiming first use in 1967, 1969, 1969, and 1974, respectively. In 1973, the word mark Caroline Emmons was also registered for use on silver polishing cloths, key rings, pens and pencils, and hand mirrors. Trademark registrations for the use of Caroline Emmons and Emmons on women's scarves and cologne were submitted in 1978 and 1979, respectively, but we have never seen any of these items.

Among the trademark registrations was one rather curious item. C. H. Stuart, Inc., filed to register "home party plan retail merchandising of costume jewelry" with the trademark Caroline Emmons in 1977, claiming a first use in commerce in 1952! Why after twenty-five years of selling jewelry using home parties did C. H. Stuart, Inc., file a trademark on the merchandising aspect of its operations? And why claim a first use in commerce of 1952, rather than 1949?

This collection of Emmons promotional items includes matches, playing cards, a luggage tag, and polishing cloths. *Courtesy of Dawn Levickas.*

Only one design mark was ever registered; it was registered in 1964, claiming first use on April 29, 1949. This design mark was used on box lids and in catalogs and other printed materials until 1969. The initial *E* with its crown was reserved to designate the Crown Collection. Crown jewelry was "handsomely boxed in rich, simulated leather. The gold-leaf *Crown E* on the cover clearly identifies your selection as something special from or for one who appreciates fine costume jewelry."

A variety of packaging.

The registered Emmons design mark.

Valuation

One of the requirements of a book like this is the inclusion of current retail prices. Jewelry pricing is very subjective. Personal tastes, current fashion trends, rarity, and condition are just some of the variables affecting the value of a piece of jewelry. In this case, we have tried to provide what we consider to be reasonable retail prices—what you might expect to pay if you were to buy the piece at an antique shop or online storefront. If you were to find that piece at an online auction or garage sale, you probably could buy it for less. But this is not always true.

In assigning values to the pieces in this book, we take into consideration the following: online auction prices, retail pricing for vintage jewelry, and personal knowledge gained from a combined 60+ years of collecting jewelry. We also add in a small amount for the escalating costs of replacing pieces. Although we appreciate when a piece comes in its original packaging, we choose not to increase value for that—you cannot wear the box!

We use a top-down approach for assigning values. That is, we first assign a price to the complete set and then use an allocation formula to assign values to the individual pieces in the set. For three-piece sets, the formula is simple: 50 percent for the necklace or brooch, 30 percent for the bracelet, and 20 percent for the earrings. In the case of a four-piece set, we assign equal values of 30 percent to the brooch and necklace and lower the value of the bracelet and earrings to 25 and 15 percent, respectively. The value of a two-piece set is broken down at 60 percent for a necklace, pin, or bracelet and 40 percent for the matching earrings. Even if part of a set, rings are always valued individually. Although these formulas provide a useful tool for assigning values, there are times when across-the-board figures from the formulas do not fit all of the pieces in a set. In these instances, the percentages are adjusted based on the quality and complexity of the individual pieces.

Since Emmons always used the term "reasonable prices" in its sales literature, adjusting original prices for inflation over the intervening years provides one way to evaluate current prices. For example, if you paid $4 for a pin in 1966 and you could sell it today for about $23, you would break even in terms of inflation. That does not mean that it is worth $23 today. Most people did not buy costume jewelry as an investment, so consider yourself very lucky if you have a piece that is worth anywhere close to its inflation-adjusted cost to you.

Table 1: Minimum, Median, and Maximum Sales Prices for Emmons Jewelry in Selected Years, 1966-1981

Item Type	Statistic Type	Year			
		1966	1971 (Fall)	1976 (Spring)	1981 (Spring)
Bracelet	Minimum	$2.25	$4.00	$7.00	$6.50
	Median	$4.50	$6.00	$9.50	$9.00
	Maximum	$5.50	$7.50	$16.00	$26.00
Earrings	Minimum	$2.50	$4.50	$5.00	$6.50
	Median	$4.00	$5.50	$7.00	$11.50
	Maximum	$7.00	$7.50	$11.50	$14.00
Necklace	Minimum	$2.25	$5.00	$5.50	$10.00
	Median	$6.00	$11.00	$13.50	$15.50
	Maximum	$8.25	$16.00	$24.00	$36.00
Pin	Minimum	$2.50	$4.50	$7.00	$8.50
	Median	$4.00	$6.25	$8.00	$10.00
	Maximum	$10.00	$12.25	$12.50	$12.50
Ring	Minimum	$3.00	$4.00	$4.50	$7.00
	Median	$3.50	$5.50	$7.00	$11.00
	Maximum	$6.25	$9.00	$10.00	$15.00

Table 1 provides some approximate values for the minimum, median, and maximum selling prices of various types of items for four years—1966, 1972, 1976, and 1981.

To find equivalent buying power in today's dollar, find the original value in the first column of Table 2 (see next page) and read across to the appropriate year column. For example, the median price for a pair of earrings in

1971 was around $5.50, as shown in Table 1. In Table 2, the value associated with the row that begins with $5.00 in the column labeled "1971" is $22.86.

Thus, based on the Consumer Price Index, it would cost you somewhere around $25 in today's dollars to buy the equivalent of $5.50 worth of 1971 goods and services. One way to think about buying power is to consider what you personally could buy today for $25 in terms of gasoline, a pair of earrings, or even your cell phone bill, especially as it relates to your total budget. Would you spend that much on high quality, fashionable jewelry if one of your friends invited you to a jewelry party at her home?

At the upper extreme, let us consider the **Cleopatra** ensemble of necklace, bracelet, and earrings (see p. 116) that sold for $30 in 1976 and to which we have assigned a current value of $76. In today's economy, your $30 in 1976 dollars would buy you almost $98 worth of goods and services. So if you buy **Cleopatra** today for $76, you've got a bargain!

Organizing a Collection

When starting a collection, display is often the collector's first concern. As the collection grows, storage becomes a factor. Eventually, maintaining records and organization become paramount. We cannot remember everything we own, and its doubtful that you can or will be able to either. Thus, you need to organize your collection using a simple, yet flexible system that allows you to determine quickly and easily if you own something or not.

Jewelry collections can be organized in a number of ways including style of design, representation themes, and physical makeup. If the collection is restricted to just one name, such as Emmons, style may not make much sense. While there are pieces representative of various styles, such as Art Deco and Victorian, such a categorization scheme quickly becomes unworkable. On the other hand, representation themes can be quite useful—up to a point. Flowers, animals, butterflies, stars, crescents, crowns, crosses, and other similar natural and manufactured objects are abundantly represented in jewelry designs. But not everything fits nicely into such a scheme. In fact, the residual would be much too large to make such a scheme practical.

Physical makeup works well with better costume jewelry where semi-precious stones are used extensively. But for the untrained eye, determining if a stone is meant to represent topaz or quartz, or is made of plastic or glass just does not make sense.

The organizational scheme we use is primarily based on color but incorporates other aspects of physical appearance, namely clear diamond-like rhinestones and pearl-like beads. Like the other schemes, this one also has its problems. Not everything is just one color; there are a variety of pearl-like beads in shapes that differ significantly from the real thing; and stones such as aurora borealis and imitation opals and moonstones defy easy categorization. One just has to set some arbitrary rules and use them.

Our classification (and rules) are as follows:

Clear (rhinestones, crystal, and aurora borealis)
Clear rhinestones and pearls
Pearls (only those closely representing cultured or freshwater pearls)
Black and shades of gray
White (including ivory and nontraditionally-shaped pearl-like beads)
Blue (including turquoise- and aqua-colored and "blue moonstone")
Green
Red, pink, and purple (including red-tinted aurora borealis)
Brown (including imitation topaz and citrine, and amber-colored stones)
Yellow, orange, and coral (excluding imitation citrine and amber-colored stones)
Multi-colored and miscellaneous (including imitation opal)
Just silver-tone
Silver- and gold-tone
Just gold-tone

Table 2: 2004 Inflation-Adjusted Values for Emmons Jewelry Purchased in Selected Years, 1966-1981*

Original Value	Original Issue Year			
	1966	1971	1976	1981
$2.50	$14.29	$11.43	—	—
$5.00	$28.58	$22.86	$16.27	$10.19
$7.50	$42.87	$34.30	$24.41	$15.28
$10.00	$57.16	$45.73	$32.55	$20.37
$12.50	—	$57.16	$40.69	$25.47
$15.00	—	$68.59	$48.82	$30.56
$20.00	—	—	$65.10	$40.75
$25.00	—	—	$81.37	$50.94
$30.00	—	—	$97.64	$61.12
$35.00	—	—	—	$71.31

* A Consumer Price Index inflation-adjusted value for any dollar amount can be found by using the "Inflation Calculator" at http://www.bls.gov/

Clear Rhinestones, Crystal, and Aurora Borealis

Pursuant to the theme "diamonds are a girl's best friend," no one seems immune to the sparkle of rhinestones. Every collection has at least one piece of jewelry featuring these brilliant stones that reflect light. Swarovski perfected the manufacture of these stones and invented the aurora borealis version in 1955. Emmons always had at least one set of rhinestone jewelry for sale, and its rhinestone jewelry made by Royal Crest featured Swarovski rhinestones.

Majestic. The bodies of the leaves are dainty filigree scrolls, and the center vein is a line of clear rhinestones. 1960s. (Necklace, 15"; Bracelet, 6.75"; Earrings, 1"). $23, $14, $9.

In this bright gold set are two bows on either side of a center rhinestone. The tails of the bows are rhinestones with each stone sitting on top of a small tag of ribbon. Each rhinestone and ribbon is a link, making these pieces very fluid. This is an older set; the earrings have screw-backs. (Necklace, 14"; Bracelet, 6.5"; Earrings, 1.5"). $31, $19, $12.

Capriccio. A golden arc split in half reveals tiny rhinestones on a field of black. The ring and earrings have the same triangular shape as in the split, with a little added gold around the edge for accent. Earrings are for pierced ears and are marked "Caroline." This is Caroline's first Limited Edition piece. It was designed by Jens Von Edler and sold only from July 1, 1977, to July 1, 1978. The mold was destroyed. (Necklace, 15"; Earrings, .75"). $30, $20. Ring, $20.

Cascade of Brilliance. Six rhinestones of various shapes and sizes are centered on a silver rope chain. 1953-55. (Necklace, 14"; Earrings, 1"). $14, $9.

Although we have not been able to identify this set by name, we feel sure it was a hostess gift or some other special issue. The rhinestones are incredibly clear and bright and are set in highly polished silver-tone arcs. The bracelet is as though the necklace has been doubled, stacking one length on top of the other. The earrings match a section of the bracelet with the addition of a larger rhinestone in the center. (Necklace, 15.5"; Bracelet, 7"; Earrings, 1"). $37, $22, $15.

Marquis-cut rhinestones are caught among fine silver threads in this set. (Necklace, 14"; Bracelet, 6.5"). $23, $15.

Crystal Lights. A large round rhinestone (.5") is surrounded by eleven small rhinestones. In the fall of 1974, this was introduced as a hostess set with a necklace and clip earrings. The ring and pierced earrings were sold separately. In the spring of 1975, the pierced earrings were added to the hostess set. The following spring, after Miss America of 1976, Tawny Godin, wore this set on her runway walk, all items were for sale. $20, $12, $8. Ring, $18.

A dazzling set where each crystal teardrop pendant is wreathed in rhinestones and falls from a crown of three clear stones. The choker chain is a rope of clear stones. We were told this was a hostess set from 1957, but we have no corroborating documentation. (Choker, 16"; Bracelet, 7"). $35, $25.

Sovereignty. A chain of gold bars and rhinestones leads to dainty gold loops separated by more rhinestones. This necklace is marked with an Emmons crown tag. The matching earrings are not quite as delicate as the necklace; the loops are much thicker than those in the necklace. 1960. (Necklace, 14"-18"; Earrings, 1.5" x .75"). $23, $15.

In the matching screw-back earrings, pendants like those in the necklace hang from—if they were diamonds—3 kt. of stone! (1.5"). $21.

Empress. Three sets of silver vines, each of their leaves set with a glittering rhinestone, are hinged together to create movement in this hostess set from the early to mid-1970s. The necklace is identified by the Emmons crown tag on the chain. (Pin/Pendant, 3" x 2"; Earrings, 2" x .75"). $32, $21.

Fire Ice. Narrow silver bands scroll among twelve clear rhinestones. All are capped with an almost heart-shaped band paved with rhinestones. Earrings not shown. 1974. (2" x 2.25"). $35.

Czarina. Silver rhinestones glitter in faux marcasite settings. Pendant not shown. 1970. (1.5"). $23.

Czarina ring. (.75"). $26.

Golden Triad. A diamond-shaped web of hammered gold-tone threads is accented with aurora borealis stones. The pendant and earrings are the same size. 1972-73. (2" x 1.25"). $20, $22.

Sparkling Beauty. The brushed edges of this broad gold leaf curl and outline twenty-five rhinestones. The matching earrings have eight rhinestones each. This was packaged in a blue and white Emmons box marked "FASHION RIGHT BAZAAR from Harpers." 1963. (Pin, 2"; Earrings, 1"). $23, $15.

Northern Lights. These gold diamond shapes, marked "EmJ," are covered with aurora borealis rhinestones. The earrings are the same size as the ring. 1959. (1.25" x .5"). $32. Ring, $23.

Rhinestones set in gold-tone metal form clusters of tiny flowers among narrow leaves. (Pin, 3" x 2"; Earrings, 1.25"). $23, $15.

The center and petals of this breathtaking golden flower are entirely covered by sparkling rhinestones. There's even a rhinestone in the base of the stem! (Pin, 2.5" x 2"; Earrings, 1"). $30, $20.

Shimmering Lace. "...feminine, lacy absolute confection of an ensemble. Its delicate tracery of leaves, all sparkling with the beauty of subdued color tones, picks up every reflection..."—*Emmons Showcase 1966*. Aurora borealis stones are set in polished silver-tone. (Pin, 3.5" x 2.5"; Earrings, 1.25" x .5"). $35, $24.

Fireworks. Three tiers of etched silver arcs, each tipped with a single rhinestone, swirl from a circle of eight rhinestones. The earrings have a slightly larger center circle with a single tier of rhinestone-studded silver arcs. (Pin, 2.25"; Earrings, 1"). $26, $17.

Like a swirling galaxy, this silver-tone set adorned with bright, round rhinestones twinkles in the light. Interestingly, the pin is marked "Emmons," one of the earrings is marked "EmJ," and the other earring is unmarked. Pin and earrings are the same size. (2.25" x 2"). $16, $23.

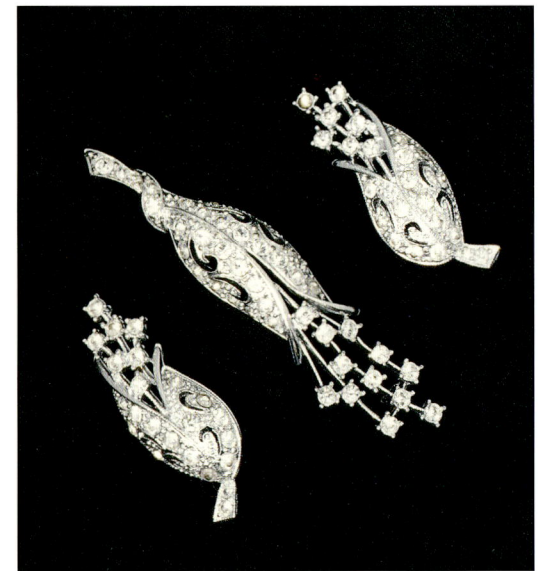

A silver-tone bud covered with glittering rhinestones sends forth a spray of even more tiny stones. (Pin, 3"; Earrings, 1.75"). $27, 18.

Sparklets. Dainty golden snowflakes covered in clear rhinestones. The earrings have screw-backs. Advertised in *Harpers Bazaar*, January 1953, 35. (Pin and Earrings, 1"). $14, $22.

These crystal daisy-like flowers are formed by surrounding a large rhinestone with eight marquis-shaped rhinestones. The pin/pendant and earrings are each 1" in diameter. $12, $19.

Stardust. "A flowing ribbon of glitter lends a gala look to the graceful design of this pin covered in tiny rhinestones."—*Emmons Showcase 1966*. (Pin, 1.25"; Earrings, .75"). $24, $20.

Crystal Leaf. "Like a delicate tendril, tipped with dew, a golden furl is capped with shimmering rhinestones."—*Emmons Showcase 1966*. (Pin, 2"; Earrings, 1"). $24, $16.

Small leaves covered in rhinestones sit on top of large shiny gold leaves with etched veins. (Pin, 2" x 1"; Earrings, 1.75" x 1"). $23, $15.

Starburst. A burst of clear rhinestones gives this set its name. The pin is marked "EmJ." (Pin, 1.25"; Earrings, 1.5" x 1.25"). $25, $17.

Four paisley motifs are crafted from golden wires and joined together to form a circle. Each is filled with leafy branches and clear rhinestone berries. (2"). $26.

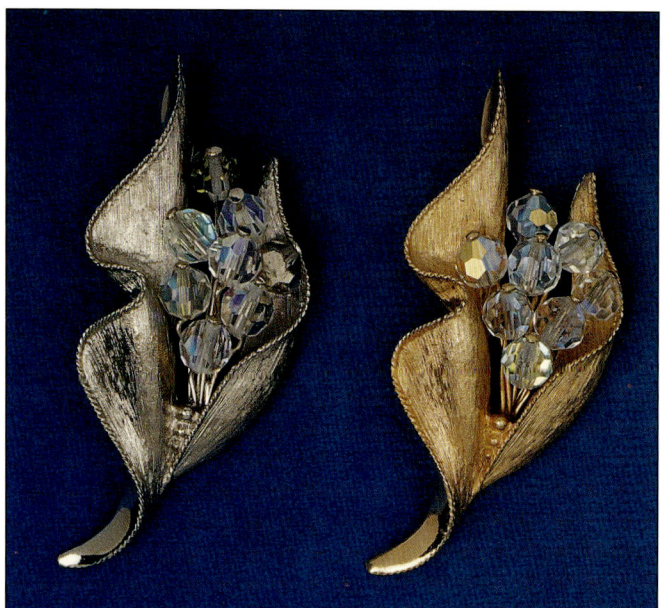

Based on a copyright description from 1963, we believe this pin is **Crystal Spray.** A curl of leaves in brushed gold-tone surrounds a spray of aurora borealis crystal beads. We have found no documentation for the silver version. (2.75"). $24 ea.

Ice Bouquet. In addition to the stone in the center of the flower, each petal and leaf is set with two brilliant rhinestones. The entire pin glitters as though coated with ice. Earrings not shown. 1972. (2.5"). $27.

Three feathers in a combination of brushed and polished gold-tone metal are held together by a band of rhinestones. Matching earrings not shown. (2.75"). $27.

Tin Lizzy. This Model T Ford is a silver-tone outline of the car highlighted with sparkling rhinestones. 1972-73. (2.25"). $26.

A stem of rhinestones holds brushed gold leaves outlined in polished gold. Some darkening of the rhinestones has occurred in these earrings. Marked "EmJ." (1.25" x 1"). $23.

A circle of clear rhinestones hangs in front of a polished gold circle. The screw-backs are mounted on the back of a square covered in rhinestones. The earrings are unmarked. They are among the very earliest Emmons pieces. (Source: Bill Scheetz.) $27.

A .75" gold square of rhinestones hangs on a rope of even more rhinestones in these dazzling drop earrings. (2.5"). $23.

35

Sparkling rings. Left: **Dinner Hour**. A 1" mirror-like stone is the centerpiece of this silver-tone ring. 1978-79. $17. A second ring of an entirely different design but with the same name was available for several years in the mid-1960s. Top right: a dome of silver rhinestones. $17. Bottom right: a dome of aurora borealis stones. $18.

Icicle. Measuring just over .25" at the widest point and 2.75" long, these slender shapes are set with clear rhinestones forming an icicle of jewels. The earrings came in both clip and pierced. 1970-72. $23.

Soft Touch, pictured at the top, is a gentle curve of rhinestones set in the middle of a silver-tone chain. In the middle is **City Lights**; each delicate arc has a rhinestone set in the end that overlaps. The necklace at the bottom has eight tiny rhinestones set in the middle of a string of silver balls. We don't know its name, but the man in our family calls it the drain chain! (All, 17"). $18 ea.

Ice Queen. These delicate, pierced earrings are tiny ropes of clear rhinestones. Photographed in the original package. 1977. (.75"). $15.

Evening Glitter. The mound of rhinestones is 1" wide and .5" high. This ring will definitely be noticed! 1969-74. $28.

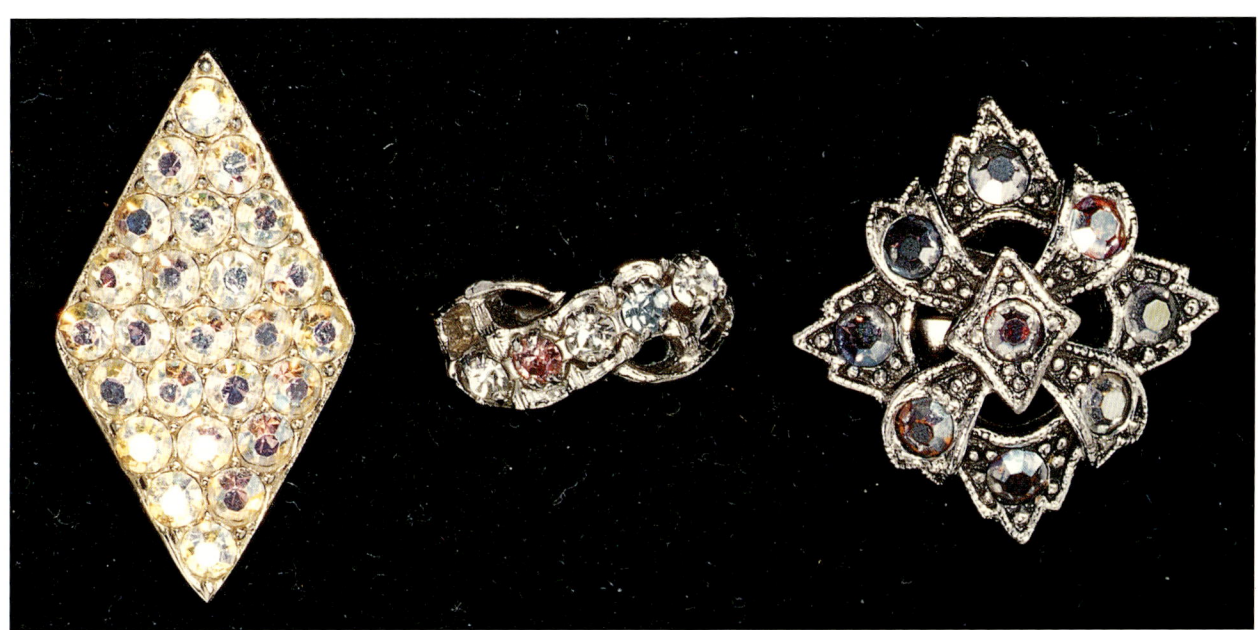

More sparkling rings. Left to right: **Northern Lights**, **Mother's Ring**, **Czarina**. The **Mother's Ring**, available from 1974 through 1977, came in five versions. This one, with one pink, one blue, and three clear rhinestones, presumably belonged to someone with one daughter and one son. $23, $18, $23.

Clear Rhinestones and Pearls

Despite the inherent beauty and sparkle associated with the combination of pearls and rhinestones, there are relatively few pieces in this category. However, two of the most popular and, therefore, longest running items are included here—**Rainbow Star** and **Starlite**.

A hostess set or other special edition of indeterminate age. Golden figure eights are set with pearls and separated by diamond shapes that each have a tiny yellow rhinestone in the center. The pearl cabochon in the pin is .75" x .5". (Necklace, 15"; Pin, 2.25" x 2"; Earrings, 1.25" x 1"). $23, $14, $9.

Queen of Fashion. This set was a Queen Hostess Gift in the mid-1960s. The pearls have depth and an almost iridescent shine. The highly polished silver leaves add to the sparkle of the rhinestones in the permanently attached enhancer. Earrings not shown. (Necklace, 16"; Bracelet, 8"). $28, $17.

Rainbow Star. The delicate gold points radiate from a center pearl and are set with tiny aurora borealis rhinestones. In 1974, the Emmons' house organ, *Timely Topics*, described this as, "Caroline Emmons' most treasured pin." To make the Vice President's Trophy, **Rainbow Star** was suspended in a block of Lucite. These trophies were given quarterly to a top manager. The set dates at least from the early 1960s and also came with pin-sized earrings (not shown). (Pin, 1.75"; Earrings, 1"). $28, $19.

Leaves decorated with golden bows tipped in pearls and aurora borealis rhinestones (one stone missing). The bows are similar in design to **Corsage** from 1960 (see next photo), but we believe this set is earlier. It is not marked. (Pin, 2" x 1.25"; Earrings, 1.5" x 1"). $20, $22.

Corsage. Pin and earrings are sprays of pearls and rhinestones emerging from double ropes joined together with golden spokes. 1960. (Pin, 2"; Earrings, 1.75"). $24, $23.

39

Sweetheart. A tiny pearl- and rhinestone-encrusted gold heart pin. 1960s. (.75"). $12.

A large (.75") pearl egg hangs from an aurora borealis rhinestone. Earrings not shown. (Chain, 15"). $18.

Starlite. A center pearl is surrounded by brushed silver-tone rays, the shorter of which are accented by aurora borealis rhinestones. This design was added to the line in 1969. In 1976, it won the famed "Swarovski Award of Excellence" given for great design in costume jewelry using their crystals. You can see the award in the picture from the 1976 *Showcase* on p. 20. This set was available throughout the 1970s. (Pin, 1.75"; Earrings, .75"). $24, $18.

Pearls

As a symbol of love, success, and happiness that can be worn with almost any costume day or night, the popularity of pearls may wax and wane, but they never really go out of style. Most of the "pearls" in Emmons jewelry are simulated or imitation pearls—plastic or glass beads covered with an iridescent coating.

A leafy branch in brushed gold with pearl berries. (Pin, 3.25" x 2.5"; Earrings, 1.25"). $24, $16.

Pearly Pinwheel. The sprays of pearls in these equal-sized pin and earrings look as though they are spinning. The set dates from the mid-1960s. (1.5"). $12, $17.

Windmill. Another version of the pinwheel shape, the "blades" in this pin are alternating textured gold and open weave. The open weave blades are studded with pearls. Early 1970s. (Pin, 2"; Earrings, 1"). $22, $16.

Classic Beauty. "…a touch of nature's own glory in double leaf pattern."—*Emmons Showcase 1965*. This lush flower is a combination of brushed and polished gold-tone petals with a pearl center. Mid-1960s. (Pin, 3"; Earrings, 1"). $23, $16.

These pearl and gold-tone metal pin and earring sets are of very similar design, but the Sarah Coventry set on the left is much larger than the Emmons set on the right. In fact, the Sarah Coventry earrings are so long that, in addition to the clip to hold the earring in place on the earlobe, a second clip is needed to hold the earring in place at the top of the ear. The Emmons set pre-dates the Coventry set. (Emmons, 1.75" x 1.25"; Sarah Coventry, 2.5" x 1") Emmons, $20, $12; Sarah Coventry, $21, $24.

Waterlily. Three layers of uplifted petals surround a pearl. (Pin, 2.5"; Earrings, 1.5"). $22, $14.

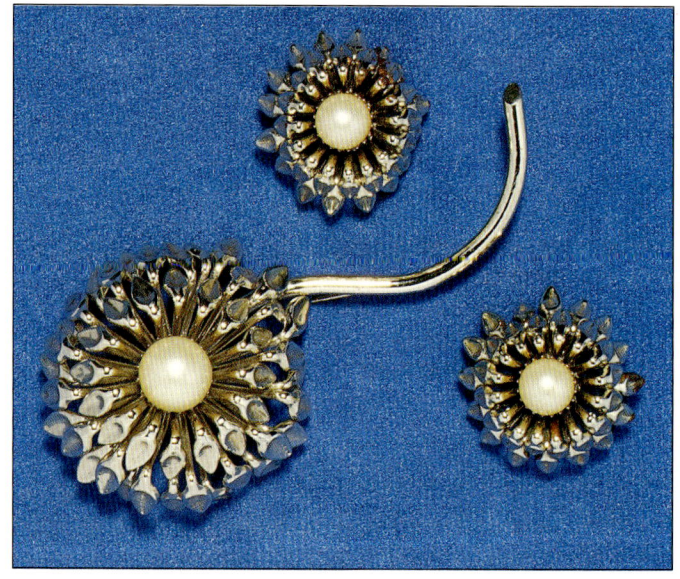

Sea Flower. Seeming to sway in an underwater current, the tips of the petals appear bent by the weight of the water. Mid-1960s. (Pin, 3.5"; Earrings, 1"). $22, $17.

Sprig of Jade. This lovely set with real Wyoming jade and cultured pearls in delicate gold-filled settings was part of the Emmons Crown Collection in 1964. (Pin, 2"; Earrings, 1"). $32, $27.

Pearly Buds. Simulated pearls drop from two pairs of gold tone leaves. 1966. (Pin, 2.75" x 1.25"; Earrings, 1"). $22, $14.

Hanging from the top of this grooved-silver circle pin are six tiny chains tipped in pearls. This set is marked "EmJ" and appears in the September 1959 ad in *Vogue* (p. 15). (Pin, 1.25" x 2"; Earrings, 1.75" x .75"). $18, $20.

My Favorite. A single pearl tipped with a tiny rhinestone hangs from a small golden flower. The overall length of the pendant is only .75". The fine chain is 16". This is another piece packaged in the blue and white Emmons box marked "FASHION RIGHT BAZAAR from Harpers." 1960s. $18, $20.

Buttercup and unknown. The earrings of wavy disks with pearl centers pre-date the **Buttercup** pendant from the mid-1970s. The pendant had a matching ring (not shown). (Pendant, .75"; Earrings, 1"). $21, $23.

Pearly Realm. Simulated pearls of varying sizes are set on golden threads in the center of the 1.5" circle. Also came in silver-tone. 1972. $21.

Blossom Time. Tiny full-blown roses with pearl centers sit on golden lace. Both the earrings and the ring are only .5" in diameter; the rosebuds themselves are a mere .25". Matching pendant not shown. 1969-70. $21. Ring, $17.

A large pearl is surrounded by two rows of smaller pearls set among golden beads. (1.5"). $23.

Filigree Flower. This pin takes its name from the silvery petals that surround the pearl. 1977. (Pin/Pendant, 2"; Chain, 22"). $26.

Two for Fashion. Left: Lovely flower with a pearl center. Right: Stylized fleur-de-lis with pearls. This set was acquired in the original packaging, another of the FASHION RIGHT BAZAAR from Harpers boxes. The original card is marked with the number 1103. 1962. (Left, 1.5"; Right, 2" x 1.5"). $17 each.

A large pearl is set in the center of swirling, silver-tone fronds. (2.5"). $21.

A large (.75") pearl is balanced on a curved gold-tone ribbon. (1.75"). $23.

A classically styled pin with two flower petals and pearl-topped stamens. Matching earrings not shown. (2.75"). $22.

Crown pin in textured gold-tone set with five pearls. (1.5" x 1.25"). $18.

Beauty Vine. A dainty bunch of tiny pearl grapes hangs from a golden vine. Mid-1960s. (1"). $18.

White Olive. Pearls are the fruit on this delicate silver olive branch. Matching earrings not shown. 1964. (2.5" x 1.75"). $23.

Scarecrow. A scarecrow in gold-toned metal with a simulated pearl for a head. 1960s. (2.5"). $24.

Sorcery (incomplete). Seven long chains tipped in pearls originally hung from this gold-tone bar pin (2") set with three pearls. Someone has removed the chains and attached four pearl beads directly to the pin. **Sorcery** was a Royal Hostess Gift during the early 1970s. $18.

Gibson Girl. This gold-tone bar pin decorated with a circle of pearls surrounding a clear rhinestone dates from the early 1960s but has the look of the 1890s. (2.5"). $18.

Two pairs of pearl earrings. Left: **Two of Hearts**. Introduced by 1969, these drop earrings of pearls in heart-shaped cages were available for much of the 1970s. Pierced earrings of the same design (not shown) were introduced in 1972. (2.5"). Right: A single pearl hangs from a pearl stud with one inch of gold "fish bones" in between. (1.5"). $16 ea.

Clusters of pearls look like bunches of grapes and hang 2" from gold clasps. $22.

Illustra. "This intriguing design...a duet of simulated pearls. Dainty and demure, 'Illustra' adds charm and simplicity to your everyday, every-occasion wardrobe."—*Emmons Showcase 1966*. Necklace not shown. (.75"). $21.

A delicate swirl of tiny silver leaves holds a pearl. (.75"). $19.

Moonlight Pearl. Simulated pearl button earrings trimmed with gold were available in the mid-1960s. The backs of these earrings are shown on p. 24. (1"). $18.

Two pearl charm bracelets. Left: A basket filled with pearls on a chain of pearls and gold beads. Marked "EmJ." Right: A pearl-filled, heart-shaped cage on a gold chain. This type of charm bracelet was quite popular in the 1950s and 1960s. $21 ea.

Plain pearl button earrings. (.75"). $14.

An adjustable bracelet of alternating links of brushed gold filigree and pearls; fits wrists up to 8". $21.

Two strands of polished gold beads and one of pearls make up this lightweight bracelet. Earrings not shown. (7"). $18.

Fashion Favorites. This string of creamy pearls, 36", can also be doubled and worn as a choker. Available from 1975-77. $27.

A collection of pearl enhancers in silver-tone. The name of the pin/enhancer with multi-colored rhinestones is unknown. $22. The smaller, round enhancer covered in jewel-tone clear cabochons and rhinestones is **Contessa** (1965). $23. The stone in the third enhancer is actually a piece of diamond-shaped glass that has been deeply etched to simulate four small diamond-shaped stones. It, too, was named **Contessa** and dates from 1966. $21. (1"-1.5").

Matchmaker. Forty-eight inches of lustrous pearls are attached to a rhinestone-encrusted scimitar clasp. The clasp is hinged and can be used to grasp the pearls in different places to create a variety of looks. Matching earrings not shown. Early 1970s. $38.

Scenario. This is a take-apart necklace. A single, heavy gold chain holds a filigree charm in the shape of an acorn (removable). Multiple gold chains, one of which has pearls along its length, are strung together to form a heavy chain. This chain has a matching bracelet that can be connected to the necklace to add length. The plain chain is 23"; the acorn is 1" x .5"; the bracelet is 6.5"; and the chain and pearl necklace is 22". Early 1970s. $32.

Cascade (incomplete). Delicate necklace of round and oblong pearl beads strung together with embossed golden bars (21"). This is one part of a two-part necklace. The 16"-18" plain chain with one set of pearl beads is missing. Also came in silver. 1976-78. $21.

Interlude. A silver-tone chain with groupings of four creamy pearls every 6.5". They are set off by silver figure 8s. The necklace comes in two parts, one 18" and the other 25.5". They may be joined together and worn as one long necklace or arranged to look like a double strand. Each section may be worn separately as well. This was also available in gold-tone, and both were sold from 1973-74. $23.

Pearlescent rice beads accent a gold chain that holds a detachable charm of pearl grapes. (Chain, 18"; Charm, 2"). $18, $8.

Prima Donna. On this necklace/belt of pearls woven through a golden chain, finer gold chains with small pearl pendants are looped from the bottom. Early 1970s. (35"). $26.

A lightweight choker with six strands of gold and pearls. (15"). $22.

Pearl rings. Left to right: **Blossom Time**. See entire set on p. 44. (.5"). $17. **Rapture**. A circle of pearls with silver filigree caps surround a raised, center pearl. Also came in gold. 1971-72. (.75"). $18. **Snowflowers**. A single pearl set in a silver lace cup is mounted on either end of this wrap-around ring. 1973-78. Pierced earrings not shown. $15.

Black and Shades of Gray

Just as stars twinkle in the midnight sky, some predominantly black jewelry items were designed for evening wear and feature rhinestones or other sparkling elements. Others fit the tailored look of suits and business wear, and some are just plain fun to wear!

Based on another copyright description, this time from 1960, we believe this is **Grand Duchess**. Pearlescent gray ovals and clusters of pearls sitting on fluted silver bases alternate along the length of the necklace and bracelet. 1960. (Necklace, 17"; Bracelet, 7"; Earrings, 1.5"). $20, $12, $12.

Jet Fantasy. The earrings of this set are dainty flowers made of faceted black and clear stones. Although the pin contains the same flower-shaped pieces, their arrangement gives it a decidedly bug-like appearance. This was a gift choice for a Royal Queen Hostess in 1969. (Pin, 2.75" x 2.5"; Earrings, 1.25"). $40, $20.

Symphonie. Graduated links of silver petals studded with bright crystals and separated by faceted black stones flow down to and through a crystal flower. Each pair of petals is like a link in a chain giving motion to these pieces. In 1963, this Queen Hostess Set was presented by Emmons' president Bill Scheetz to Miss New York State, Paula Roberta Heins. Bracelet not shown. (Necklace, 14"; Earrings, 2"). $40, $16.

Starry Night. The points of this lovely star are shiny black navettes. They radiate from an open-work silver base set with clear rhinestones, at the center of which is a round black cabochon. The earrings match one point of the star and dangle from a silver chevron set with a clear rhinestone. 1972-74. (Pin, 2.25"; Earrings, 1.75"). $28, $17.

Large, polished black teardrops are caught among silver ribbons. (Necklace, 14"; Bracelet, 7"; Earrings, .75" x .5"). $23, $14, $9.

Jet Splendor. Silver filigree frames surround ovals of black. 1965. (Bracelet, 7"; Earrings, 1.5"). $22, $14.

Long ovals of shiny black are held in sleek silver frames. (Necklace, 14"; Earrings, 1" x .5"). $21, $14.

Midnight Magic. "Jet always spells excitement and intrigue! Our own Midnight Magic possesses these qualities plus a special allure in its unbelievably light and satiny-soft chain. It has more magic, too. When you first pick it up, you have a matinee length necklace. Thru the magic of interlocking jump rings, one section of the necklace can be removed and you have a lovely matching bracelet."—*Emmons Showcase 1966*. (Necklace, 23" or 16"; Bracelet, 7"; Earrings, 2"). $19, $11, $8.

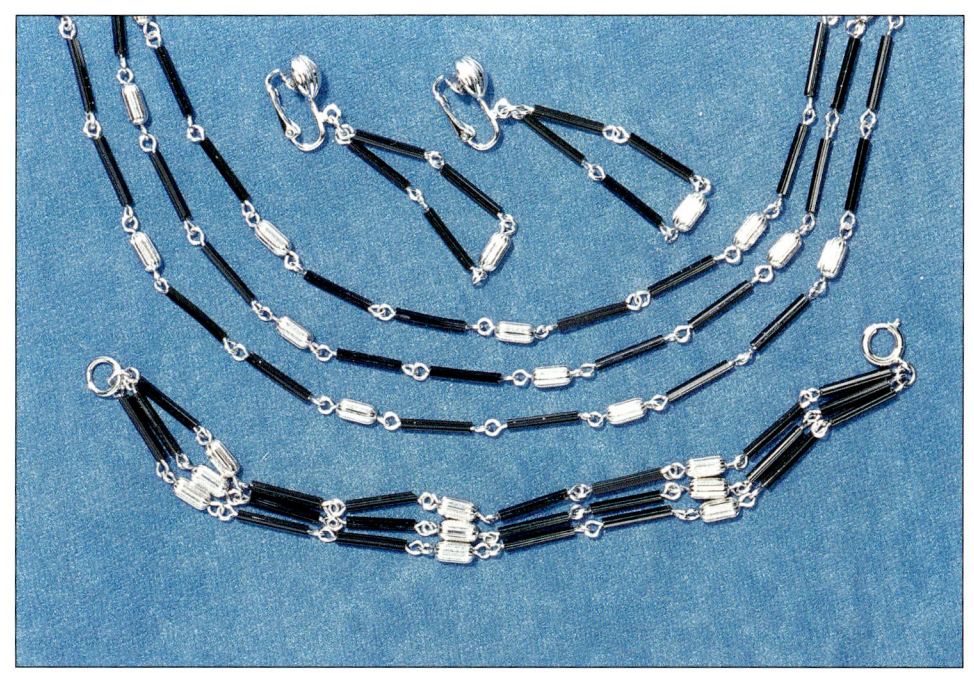

Serene Beauty. Each stone of shiny jet is etched with a delicate bow. The etching cuts below the black surface to the white interior, making it look as if the bow is an inset of mother-of-pearl. Each stone is framed by a silver band. Mid-1960s. (Pendant, 1.75"; Chain, 17"; Bracelet, 7"; Earrings, .75" x .5"). $22, $13, $9.

Ropes of faux marcasite surround shiny black ovals in a set that is very much in style today. All of the pieces are quite heavy. Bracelet and ring not shown. (Necklace, 17"; Earrings, 1"). $27, $14.

Pendulum. Three sets of graduated black beads hang from a curved bar set in the middle of the silver chain. Very 1970s! Matching earrings not shown. Also came in cream and gold. 1974. (Necklace, 14"; Pendant, 3"). $27.

Jet Cascade. Triple silver chains connect the silver-framed, smooth black stones to form this 52" *sautoir*, meaning a long, rope-style necklace. Chains are attached to the ear clips in such a way that they hang from both sides of the earlobe. Earrings are 1.5". Early 1970s. $27, $18.

Mobility. A shiny silver cage holds a bar of faux onyx. The 2.5" x .75" pendant hangs from 24" of silver chain. The earrings are miniatures of the pendant, measuring only 1" x .25". This set also came in gold and white. 1976-77. $28, $14.

Jet Elegance (incomplete). This 44" chain holds filigree frames containing faceted jet ovals. The matching earrings are individual frames hanging from a filigree round. The necklace was introduced in the fall of 1973; earrings (both pierced [not shown] and clip) were introduced one year later. This set came with a second chain (not shown). The bracelet (not shown) of the same name has oval filigree pieces instead of rectangular. Both this and the gold version with topaz stones (shown on p. 103) were customer favorites, appearing in catalogs for four years. $20, $13.

Topping each textured gold section of the necklace is a prong-set, gray glass oval surrounded by pearls. The oval is faceted in such a way that when you look into it, you see a star. We have two, one with three sections and one with four. We think the three-section version is as designed. We base this on a handwritten note on the back of the card that came with the longer necklace that reads, "1 x link added." Both original cards are marked 3585/N. However, since the altered necklace has additional connecting links that match the originals, we believe this might have been a special order. (Necklace, 12" or 15"; Earrings, 1.25" x 1"). $27, $18.

Southern Stars. This hostess set was inspired by Holiday on Ice of 1962. The beads in the three-strand necklace are very unusual. They are black with metallic gold spots around the circumference. A spiky, white star appears at both ends of the beads. These beads are strung alternately with faceted aurora borealis crystal beads. While the necklace shows off the gold in the beads, the earrings highlight the stars. (Necklace, 17"; Earrings, 1"). $38, $23.

Golden Veil. The black ovals are covered with a web of fine golden threads that make the stones look almost like crackle glass. (Pendant, 1.5"; Earrings, .75"). $17, $22.

Golden Veil ring. $19.

Sea Beauty. This silver flower of the sea has a domed center stone surrounded by spiky petals of marcasite. Early 1970s. (Pin, 2.25"; Earrings, 1"). $20, $23.

Bewitching. A simple, classy set of hematite teardrops. The stone in the necklace is 1" x .75", and those in the earrings are .75" x .5". 1969. $18, $22.

Tightly wound ribbons of gold form swirling plumes accented with gray pearls. (Pin, 2.25"; Earrings, 1"). $20, $13.

Crown Jewel. Reminding us of an elaborate compass rose, the black cabochon is topped by a gold star with a rhinestone center making it twinkle. In turn, the star is surrounded by alternating clear rhinestones and seed pearls. Every other golden ray of the collar is a fleur-de-lis. Marked "EmJ." 1953-56. (1"). $24, $27.

Fashion Tracery. Lightweight painted open-work metal sets described in the 1970s era catalogs as "…refreshing as the gentle breezes." This set has layered petals of black and silver. Other color combinations seen later in the book are white and gold, pink and gold, and burgundy and orange. (Pin, 2.5"; Earrings, 1.25"). $22, $15.

Iridescent glass seashells and smooth, black ocean pebbles are tossed in waves of silver. Marked with an Emmons crown tag. Matching bracelet and earrings not shown. $22.

Black Magic. This reversible pendant looks like a golden tassel from one side. However, flip it over, and you have an amazing step-faceted black-glass stone. 1963. (Pendant, 2" x 1.25"; Chain, 24"). $35.

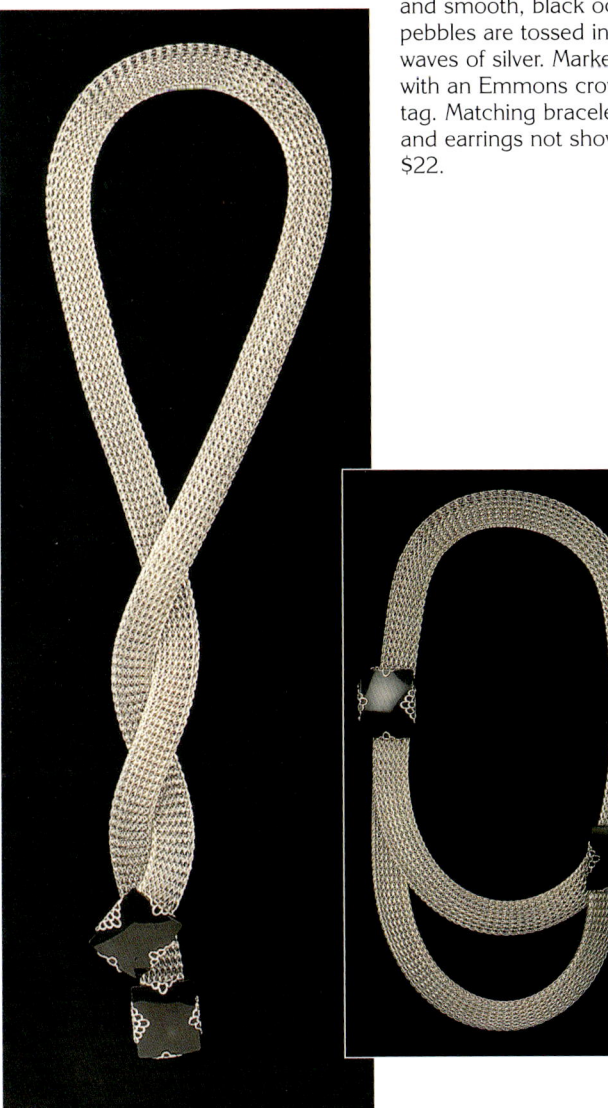

Spellbinder. "It's a belt...It's a necklace...It's a Cleopatra arm-bracelet! Soft, smooth mesh metal. Magic hooks hold the jet clasps wherever it pleases you for 'do you own thing' fashion-magic." —*Caroline Emmons Showcase Christmas 1971*.
Spellbinder was offered well into the 1970s. A white and gold version of this necklace/belt was available from 1969 through spring/summer 1978. The white earrings (p. 74) were also sold beginning in 1969, but were taken out of the line after the 1973 spring/summer catalog. Black earrings matching the clasps were introduced in spring/summer 1973, but that was the only time they appeared in a catalog. Emmons introduced its Boutique Collection in the fall of 1974, and **Spellbinder** became part of this collection. Earrings not shown. (36" x .75"). $39.

Midnight Butterfly. An enameled black butterfly on a gold chain that adjusts from 15" to 17" was introduced in the spring of 1978, and that fall pierced earrings, a stickpin, and a ring were added (none shown). It was last offered in 1981. (1.25" x .75"). $16.

Left: **Onyx and Lace**. Right: Name unknown. Both of these are from the Emmons Crown Collection, which means the onyx stones are genuine, as is the diamond chip in the piece on the right. The settings are 1/20 12 kt. gold-filled. Both date from the 1960s. (.5"). $24 ea.

Jet Petite. An elegant bracelet of onyx ovals set in gold. There was also a version in white (not shown). This 1966 bracelet should not be confused with the **Jet Petite** line that came out in the mid-1970s. (6.5"). $19.

Golden Dynasty. Polished geometric shapes add texture to the tops of the black stones in this sleek, gold bracelet. Earrings and ring not shown. 1973. (7"). $17.

A brushed-aluminum leaf accented with a gray pearl is covered in shiny silver speckles that look like splashes of rain. Earrings not shown. (1.5"). $17.

Lambie Pie. This dear little black sheep has a green rhinestone eye and lots of curly golden fleece. 1972. (1.75" x 1.5"). $24.

Indian Summer. Black was one of the colors added after the initial launch of this collection in goldenrod, beige, green, cinnamon, and rust. See p. 90 for a full description of these sets (green, p. 90; beige, p. 108; goldenrod, p. 112) Necklace not shown. 1977-78. (2"). $12.

Flamenco. Golden charms dangle from slender black beads. Matching necklace and pierced earrings not shown. 1976. (1.75"). $17.

Mystique. Ribbons of gold surround hematite centers, the properties of which are probably what inspired the intriguing name of these earrings. Mid-1960s. (1.25"). $23.

Faceted hematite rounds sit on top of three gold interlocking rings. (1"). $23.

Simple black ovals in smooth silver frames. They appear to match the **Jet Petite** bracelet shown on p. 60, but we find no mention of matching earrings in any of our documentation. (.5"). $16.

Collection of black stone rings. Top down, from the 12 o'clock position: **Dazzler**, a faceted hematite stone set on a wide hammered-silver band, 1978-81, $16; **Jet Classic**, black ovals in simple bands, silver left and gold right, $19 ea.; **Saturn**, a faceted glass stone surrounded by smaller channel-set stones in a gold setting, 1976, $23; a black stone with a white stripe set in a very simple gold setting, $12; and **Evening Glamour**, an odd-shaped stone lined down one side with rhinestones and silver swirls, $21.

Another view of **Evening Glamour**. "'Evening Glamour' is the ring you'll choose when you're dressed your best."—*Emmons Showcase 1965*. We chose to spotlight this ring because it was one of the longest-running items we have been able to document, being offered from at least the early 1960s through 1980. (1.25"). $21.

White

If stately elegance is the predominate feeling engendered by the last category, *joie de vivre* prevails here. With flowers and white beads designed to accessorize summer wardrobes, ivory and pearl-like pieces provide year-round elegance.

Gay Capri. Golden arcs surround bright, white mother-of-pearl disks that are topped with tiny gold flowers with rhinestone centers. Introduced in 1956. (Necklace, 14"-16"; Bracelet, 7"; Earrings, 1"). $30, $18, $12.

White enameled flowers with raised golden centers. Each blossom is 1.75". (Necklace, 14"-16"; Bracelet, 6.75"; Earrings, 1.25"). $22, $13, $9.

Royal Rose. A golden vine with carved ivory flowers and clear rhinestones. 1961. (Necklace, 14"; Bracelet, 7"; Earrings, 1"). $16, $9, $6.

White plastic flowers have pearl centers and delicate golden stamens. The matching earrings are marked "EmJ." (Necklace, 15"; Earrings, 1.5"). $20, $13.

White Camellia. "The delicate molding of white petals outlined in golden shadows is most striking!"—*Emmons Showcase 1966*. (Pin, 2.5"; Earrings, 1.5"). $18, $12.

Blooming Dogwood. Three white dogwood blossoms on a single gold-tone stem. 1963. (Pin, 3.5" x 2"; Earrings, 1"). $29, $16.

In this poinsettia-like, two-layered flower, the lower petals are gold-tone; the smaller, upper petals are of white enamel and surround a large pearl. (Pin, 2.5"; Earrings, 1.25"). $17.

Large enameled daisies with textured gold-tone button centers. Pin and earrings are the same size. (2"). $21, $23.

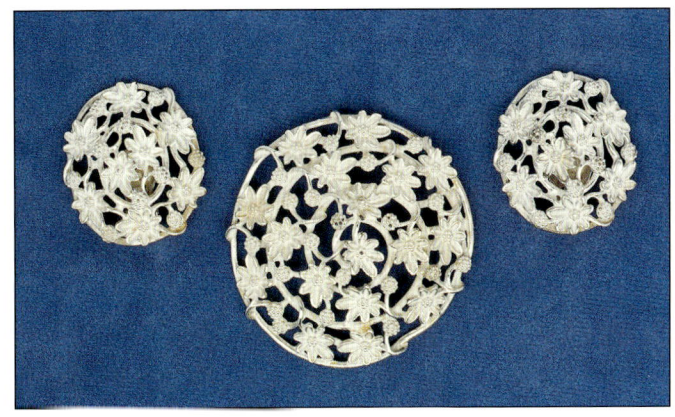

Painted white blossoms climb along the silver-tone spiral trellis. (Pin/Pendant, 2.5"; Earrings, 1.5"). $21, $19.

Fashion Tracery. Open work pinwheel-like flowers with layered petals of white and gold. Other examples of this design are found throughout the book. Early 1970s. (Pin, 2.5"; Earrings, 1.25"). $22, $15.

Magic Lantern. At the ends of this 36" textured gold chain are delicate lanterns, the interiors of which are mother-of-pearl. There is a small pearl at the top and bottom of the lanterns and stacked gold balls hang from the bottom pearl. The earrings hang from a larger pearl framed in gold rope. The lanterns are 2" long. The bracelet is 7.25" long. This was one of the first designs to be copyrighted (1959) and was worn by Lee Remick in the movie *Anatomy of a Murder*. By 1964, only the necklace remained in the catalog. The earrings are marked "EmJ"; the necklace has the rectangular Emmons copyright tag. $30, $23, $22.

Confection (incomplete). Necklace and bracelet of pearly disks held together by golden links. The bracelet is a double strand. The missing pendant is a larger version of the bead in the earrings, shown above right. Mid-1960s. (Necklace, 34"; Bracelet, 7"). $20, $12.

Confection. Large, lightweight pearlescent beads with a swirl design hang from grooved golden balls. (1.75" x .5"). $12.

Pearl Glamour. "…The tear-drop styling of this pretend pearl on a graceful chain gives it a soft delicate look…"—*Emmons Showcase 1965*. (Pendant, 1.5"; Earrings, 1.25"). $18, $12.

A single leaf (2" x 1.25") carved from mother-of-pearl with etched lines forming veins hangs from a 14" snake chain. $18.

Iridescent Rainbow. White pillow-like stones pick up a rainbow of colors in their gold wire settings. 1960s. (Necklace, 16"; Earrings, 1"). $18, $12.

Spangle Dangle. Seven strands with two white rice beads each hang from a 2.25" gold filigree oval with a white cabochon center. Offered only in the spring of 1973, it also came in silver-tone with red, white, and blue stones (not shown). (Necklace, 30"; Earrings, 1.75"). $23, $15.

Tropicana. The stems of nine brushed gold leaves fold around a chain of pearly, tumbled nuggets. 1959. (Necklace, 16; Earrings, 1.25" x .75"). $21, $14.

Thin, wavy white and beige disks are strung closely together to make ruffled "beads." Bracelet not shown. (Necklace, 14"; Earrings (one missing), 1.25"). $17, $11.

Off-white plastic rice beads hang in the centers of what resemble little golden horseshoes with the ends pointing up so the luck won't run out. Bracelet not shown. (14"). $22.

Fourteen graceful, enameled white leaves trimmed in gold hang from this 17" necklace marked with an Emmons crown tag. Earrings not shown. $18.

Lite 'n Brite. "Gossamer strands … light in weight … bold in beauty—caress your neck in an exciting treatment of Emmolite …" –*Emmons Showcase 1965*. Shown in white with silvery finish, it also came in white with a golden finish. Mid-1960s. (17"). $15.

Three strands of big, bold pearlescent white round and oval beads are separated with gold spacer beads. The oval beads have deeply carved swirls. These match the single strand shown below. (20"). $28.

Bright white balls and grooved oval beads alternate in this 18" necklace. The hook clasp is marked Emmons. Also came in black. Earrings not shown. $15.

This necklace has one double chain in gold and a single strand of linked milky disks. Someone has removed the pearl-like coating from the disks. This necklace cannot be divided into separate pieces as so many others can. (Plain chain, 30"; Chain with disks, 26"). $27.

Midas Touch. The two 50-inch strands can be worn together or separated into two necklaces. Early 1970s. $32.

This double-chain necklace has a removable pendant. One chain is silver, the other white. Six tiny white beads dangle from the large white ball on chains of white and silver. (Necklace, 14"; Earrings, 2"). $18, $12.

We have no documentation for this but, based on its overall length of 38", we think it might be a necklace/belt. The double chain, one with links smaller than the other, holds frosted gray and white beads. There is a removable pendant of two beads that should have at least one more bead, probably two. Four chains make up the other tassel; however, one white bead is missing. $22.

Honey Bunny. A funny, not-so-little bunny pendant, he's 3.5" of white enamel with swinging golden eyes and a dangling gold tail. He also came in all gold. He was part of the Boutique Collection in 1975-76. $27.

Sixteen golden rays radiate from a white plastic cabochon on this pin/pendant. The tip of each ray is a white flower with a clear rhinestone center. Judging by the type of pin back, this is an early piece. Its number is 4815. (2"). $26.

This pin has a translucent, white wash over a swirl of honey-combed gold. Earrings not shown. (2"). $21.

Coquette is a pin from 1966. Almost a flower in its own right, the golden center sits upon lush, white enameled petals. Earrings not shown. (1.75"). $21.

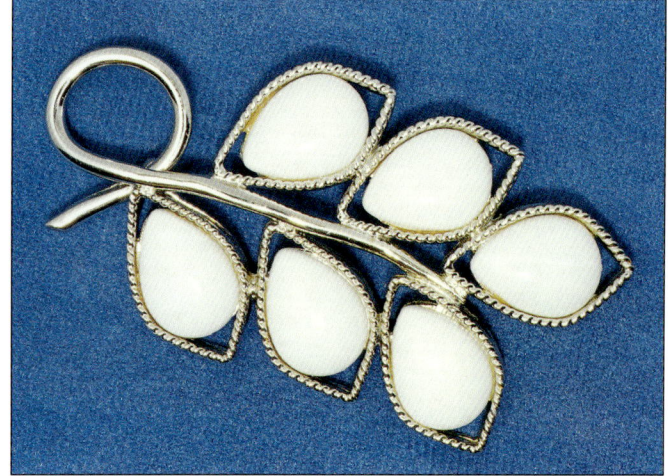

Snow Queen. Three inches of gold, open-work leaves with white plastic teardrop centers. 1964. (3"). $24.

Starburst. A crimped gold-tone setting holds white plastic stones. Watch for this pin in different colors in other chapters of the book! Earrings not shown. 1971. (Pin, 2.75"). $24.

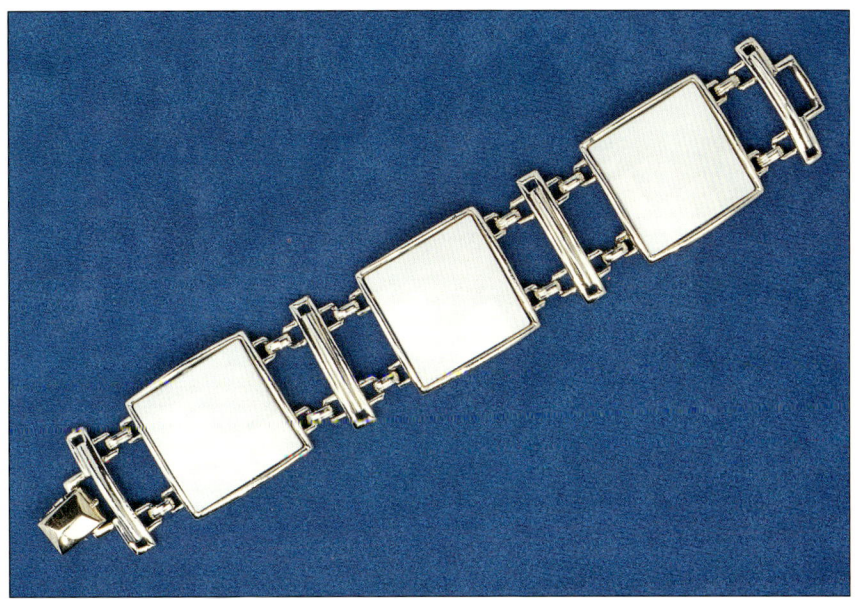

In this gold bracelet, large plastic squares have been molded to look faceted. Each is a generous one square inch. (7"). $23.

In this bracelet numbered 4678, sprays of bright gold are accented with tiny gold beads framing white plastic buttons. Marked "EmJ." Necklace and earrings not shown. (7"). $23.

Turnabout. A reversible bracelet of heavy filigree squares with a white stone on one side and silvery swirls on the other. 1962. (7"). $24.

Giant mother of pearl "E" shapes are linked together to form this fun bracelet marked "EmJ." Earrings not shown. (7.25" x 1"). $27.

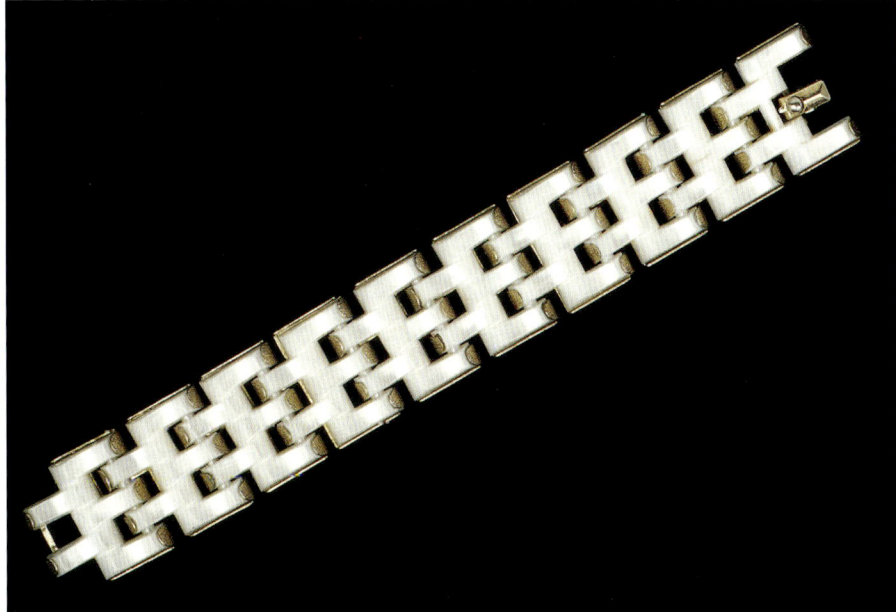

White Classic. An unusual white stone is framed in gold and perches on three golden bands. 1977. (.75"). $17.

Festival. A 1" white cabochon hangs in a brushed gold circle from which five white beads drop. Matching pendant not shown. Available for only a short time in 1972. A two-piece chain necklace with colored beads was introduced in 1975 using the same name. (1.5"). $21.

Spellbinder. These mother-of-pearl rectangles wrapped in gold filigree and marked "EmJ" are part of the gold-tone version of this set. (Necklace not shown.) The set also came in silver with black and is fully pictured and described on p. 59. The white and gold earrings were available from 1969 through spring/summer of 1973, while the necklace/belt was available until the spring/summer of 1978. Both sets became part of Emmons' Boutique Collection when it was introduced in the fall of 1974. (1" x .75"). $18.

White Cap. Anchored in the centers of golden oval frames are .5" white cabochons. Matching ring not shown. 1974-75. (1.25"). $21.

74

Blue and Turquoise

Blue has always been one of the most popular colors in jewelry. Sapphire, blue topaz, lapis lazuli, aquamarine, turquoise, blue moonstone, and blue zircon all belong to the family of blue gemstones. Despite the range in color these natural gemstones represent, most Emmons pieces fall into only two groups: blue rhinestones (à la blue topaz or blue zircon) and simulated turquoise. There are also a few stunning examples of non-gemstone blue jewelry.

A single baby blue rhinestone accents bright silver petals. (Pin, 3"; Earrings, 2"). $22, $15.

Blue Swirl with Tassels (incomplete). Deep aqua rhinestones are the centerpieces in this pin of joined concentric circles. The pin was originally accented with three gold chains. Matching necklace and bracelet not shown. 1953-54. (Pin, 2"; Earrings, 1"). $26, 18.

Blue Rhapsody. Silver-tone star covered in blue aurora borealis rhinestones. Earrings match the center of the star pin. 1966. (Pin, 1.75"; Earrings, .5"). $35, $23.

Blu-Bud. "Oh, flower fair, so bright and clear, by day or night, Your aqua blossom, bold and beauteous shines forth in sheer delight. Your silv'ry petals and shining stem reflect the sun's bright rays. Blu-Bud you are the pin for me to wear on happy days!"– *Emmons Showcase 1965*. (Pin, 2.5"; Earrings, 1"). $22, $14.

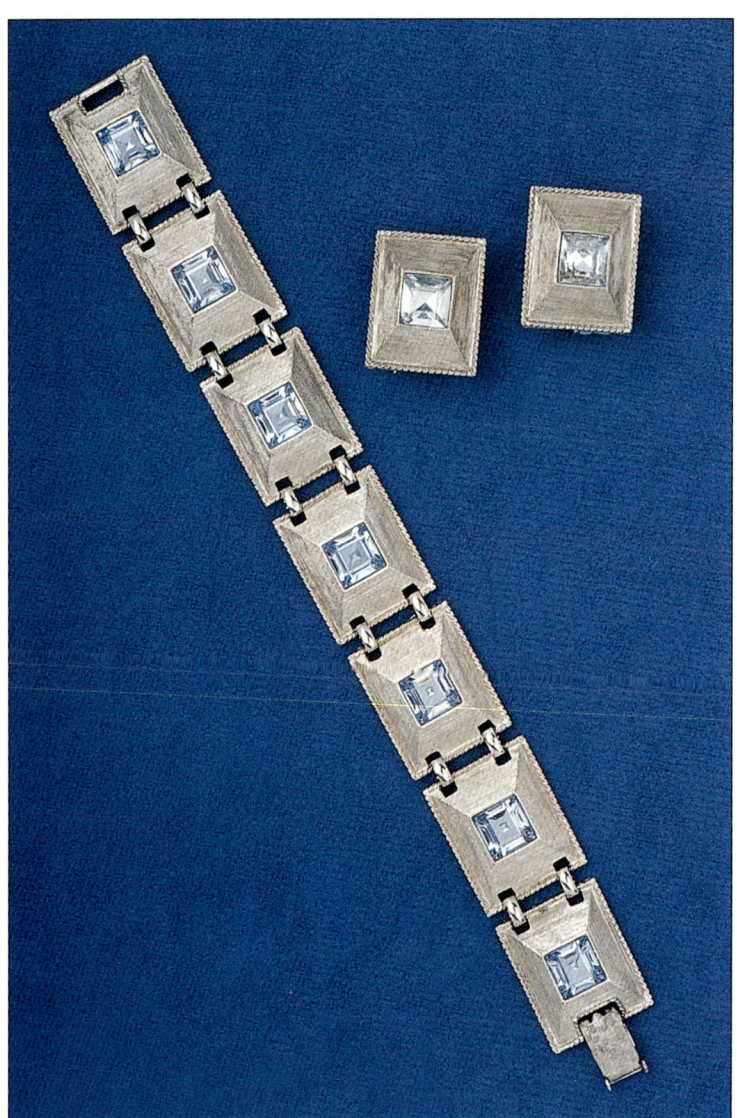

Caprice. A bar pin of silver filigree set with seven light blue rhinestones. 1975. (2.75"). $19.

Square, sky blue rhinestones sit atop brushed silver pyramids. Each pyramid in the bracelet and the earrings is 1" x .75". Because the gold backing is missing, the stones in the earrings are considerably lighter than those in the bracelet. (6.75"). $22, $14.

This unmarked snowflake-shaped pin in gold-tone with pale blue rhinestones came on its original card showing item number 1104. Earrings not shown. (1"). $21.

A large-link silver chain is outlined by baby blue rhinestones on both sides at the center of the chain. Marked "EmJ." (14"). $27.

Dainty crescent earrings of three graduated baby blue rhinestones accented with a tiny clear rhinestone. (.75"). $16.

Blue Ice. Two-tone (pale blue and yellow) faceted glass squares set in golden baskets. When looking into the stone, the rayed medallion on the setting underneath looks like a small blue flower. 1960. Ring not shown. (.75"). $33.

Brushed silver outlines of leaves are filled in with deep blue marquis-shaped and light blue round-shaped rhinestones. Pin not shown. (1.5"). $22.

Smooth stones in clear sky and royal blues nestle together against a silver divider and are framed by silver-tone ropes. Ring not shown. (1"). $21.

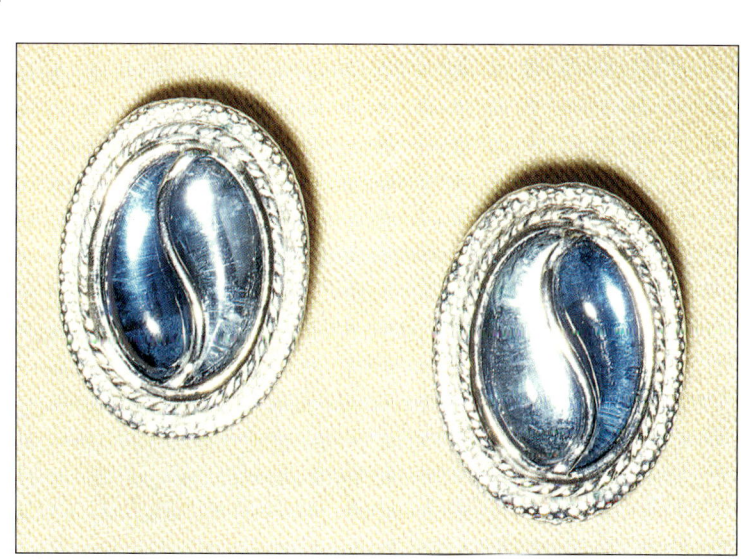

77

Wedgewood Cameo. A tiny cameo on pale blue is surrounded by very bright rhinestones, and all are caught up in a ribbon of gold. Marked "EmJ." Mid-1950s. (1"). $23.

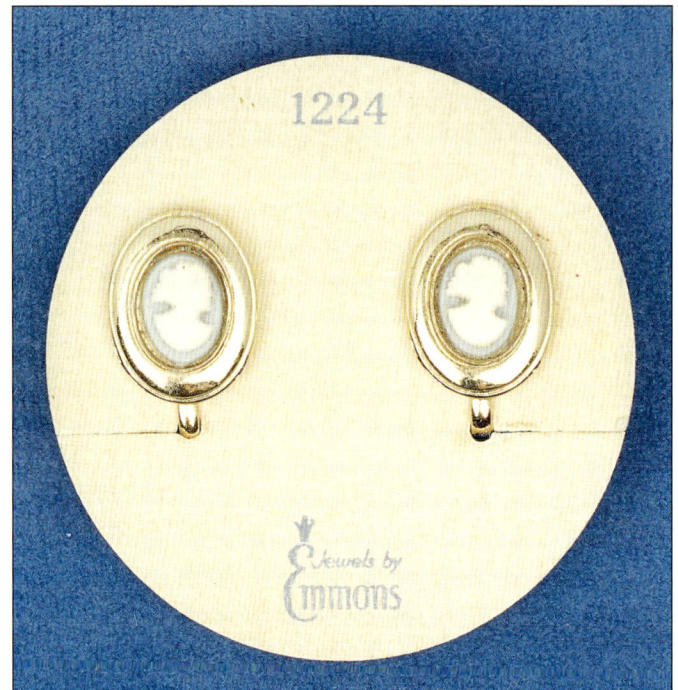

Wedgewood Cameo. The centers of these golden oval, screw-back earrings are cameos on a pale blue background. The card they came on shows the number 1224. Mid-1950s. (.5"). $17.

Misty Blue. This piece takes its name from the large, foggy, peacock blue cabochons set in silver filigree and accented with pearls. 1969. (Pin, 2"; Earrings, 1.25"). $24, $16.

Bluebell. Slender flower pin with blue cat's-eye cabochons framed in roughened silver that shines as though paved with rhinestones. (Pin, 3"; Earrings, 1"). $23, $15.

Blue Fire. For her, cabochons of clear royal blue with mirror-like backings are set in simple, scalloped gold frames in this set of ring and earrings. Both earrings are marked "Emmons," and the ring is unmarked. Stones are 1" x .5". 1960. $21 ea.

Elaborate silver-tone settings hold square stones of marbled blue shot with gold. The set is further accented with small black beads standing sentinel over the center stones. (Bracelet, 6.5"; Earrings, 1.25"). $24, $16.

Blue Fire. For him, the same cabochons are used in cufflinks and tie bar. We have two tie bars. One is marked "EmJ"; the other is unmarked. One cufflink is marked with what may be an "E," and the other is unmarked. The card the tie bar came on is dated 1960 and shows the number 4825. Stones are 1" x .5". $21 ea.

Accented by bold slashes of silver, this heavy set is made of deep blue stones, possibly ceramic, with a matte finish. The surface has been splattered with a shiny material that changes from aqua to deep purple, depending on the light. (Bracelet, 6.5"; Earrings, 1"). $27, $18.

Triangles, upon triangles, upon triangles in this bracelet with "stones" of molded white and deep blue plastic framed with beaded silver wire. (7" x 1.25"). $21.

Indian Princess. Faux turquoise stones set in the style of a Navajo squash blossom necklace and marked with a round Emmons tag. Mid- to late 1970s. (Necklace, 17"; Earrings, 1"). $24, $16.

Mexicana. Elongated ovals of faux turquoise outlined in silver rope. The bracelet and ring are further accented with darkened silver scallops. The ring was introduced in 1972, the bracelet added in 1976, and the pierced earrings and necklace in 1978. Necklace not shown. (Bracelet, 2.5" dia.; Decoration, 1.5" x .5"; Earrings, 1"; Ring, .75" x .5"). $20, $12, $8.

A pin with the look of a golden sea urchin is accented with turquoise beads. (Pin, 2"; Earrings, 1.75" x .75"). $23, $15.

You can almost hear the whisper of a soft, tropical breeze as it passes over this slender, silver-tone leaf enameled in aqua. (Pin, 3.5"; Earrings, 1.5"). $20, $13.

Garden Party. Among the silver swirls of this pin, enameled blue flowers and green leaves are accented with turquoise beads. This set also came in gold with white enameled flowers and peach and yellow bead accents. 1973. (Pin, 2.5"; Earrings, 1"). $21, $14.

Renaissance. A marbled turquoise cabochon surrounded by a circle of turquoise beads set in antiqued gold fancywork. Earrings not shown. 1968. (1.75"). $28.

Crowning Glory. Alternating circular rows of turquoise beads and pearls set in gold-tone metal with a slightly raised center. Earrings not shown. 1963. (2"). $23.

Delft Romance. Large white rice beads decorated with delicate blue roses are strung along a 53" silver chain. An 18" section with one bead may be separated and worn as a shorter necklace. Matching earrings are 1.25" and also came in a pierced version (not shown). 1976-77. $18, $12.

Fantasy Circles. A variegated blue disk hangs in the center of two concentric circles in silver-tone. The circles and disk spin independently. 1977-78. (Pendant, 3"; Chain, 20"). $23.

Fashion Crusader (incomplete). Antiqued gold-tone cross set with turquoise beads and pearls with a large deep blue rhinestone at the center. Chain not shown. Early 1970s. (2.75" x 1.75"). $24.

Turquoise beads are set with white pearls among tiny silver beads and twisted silver threads. It is marked by an Emmons crown tag. Designed to be worn at 14". $32.

Simple earrings in gold with a round turquoise bead hanging from a half turquoise bead. (.75"). $16.

Aztec Princess. A lacy silver circle is split at the top where the edges are curled over to form a channel for the double chain. The turquoise cabochon is surrounded by tiny brushed silver flowers with bead centers. The tassel on the bottom is removable. 1972. (Pin/Pendant, 1.75" x 1.5"; Tassel, 2"; Chain, 28"). $30.

Roman Holiday (incomplete). This is one-third of a fill-in necklace hostess set. The double silver-tone chain has two offset sections consisting of a large link flanked by slivers of hammered metal. The pendant is a large turquoise dome set upon a collar etched with rays. In the line from the early 1970s, **Roman Holiday** was taken out of the hostess gift category in 1974, given a new number, and sold for $25 as part of the first Boutique Collection. $23.

Leap Frog. A small silver frog has bulging turquoise bead eyes. Early 1970s. (1.75"). $24. **Springtime.** In gold-tone, a tiny bird with a red glass eye stands on a branch next to a nest containing three turquoise bead eggs. Mid-1960s. (2" x 1.25"). $24.

Blue Reverie. Antiqued-silver open-work pyramids, each topped with five turquoise beads. Earrings, pin, and ring not shown. 1973. (6.5"). $23.

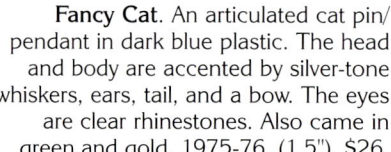

Fancy Cat. An articulated cat pin/pendant in dark blue plastic. The head and body are accented by silver-tone whiskers, ears, tail, and a bow. The eyes are clear rhinestones. Also came in green and gold. 1975-76. (1.5"). $26.

A collection of owls. Left to right: Small silver owl earring has a marbled turquoise, white, and shiny copper cabochon body and tiny turquoise rhinestone eyes. (1"). $14. **Mr. Who-o.** A gold owl whose oversized turquoise eyes give him a startled look; his body is a marbled turquoise and white cabochon. 1971. (2"). $24. **Hootie.** He's sitting on an antiqued silver-tone branch. His feathers are carved in his dark blue body, and his eyes are bright blue rhinestones. He also came in marbled brown on a gold branch (p. 108).

Aztec Lace. An open-work silver ring set with black and turquoise stones. Matching pierced earrings not shown. 1974-76. (1" x .75"). $18.

A turquoise stone set in a wide, hammered-silver band. $18.

Turquoise cabochon with patches of white and shot with gold. $16.

The high setting (.5") hides the fact that the stone spins to show turquoise on one side and coral on the other. You will see the other side of this ring in the section on coral (p. 114). $32.

Moon Shadows. This large ring, a domed moonstone surrounded by silver filigree, was available from the early to mid-1970s. (1" x .75"). $22.

Moon Mist. A blue moonstone set in gold. The matching earrings and pendant are not shown. 1966. $17.

Shalimar. White, oval moonstone surrounded by a delicate silver frame set with aurora borealis blue rhinestones. 1973-74. (1.25"). $24.

Green

Emmons sold only a few pieces of green rhinestone jewelry over the years. However, there is an astounding diversity in types and colors of "stones"—from jelly bean and avocado green plastic cabochons to imitation carved jade medallions and smoky green, faceted glass stones.

Camelot. Light and dark green marquise-shaped rhinestones set in Florentine gold-tone swirls. Mid-1960s. (Pin, 2"; Earrings, .75"). $23, $12.

Each petal of this cushiony flower is tipped with three silver balls. The petals surround a center of ten emerald green rhinestones. (Pin and Earrings, 1.75"). $16, $24.

Gay Marguerita. "Scintillating Marguerita stones are the highlight of this jewelry bouquet."—*Emmons Showcase 1965*. Tied with a gold ribbon, the flowers are watermelon rivoli-cut glass, and there is a tiny rhinestone in the center of each one. 1960s. (Pin, 2" x 1.5"; Earrings, 1"). $40, $27.

Duchess. An emerald-cut, smoke green stone (1") is surrounded by a corona of gold. Matching earrings have a .75" stone. 1963. $33, $22.

A sprig of gold-tone leaves accented by cat's-eye-like emerald green stones. (Pin, 2.75"; Earrings, 1.25"). $30, $20.

Funflowers. A pin and earrings with bright lime green enameled petals and lemon yellow plastic centers. Yellow and orange versions shown on p. 109. 1969. (Pin, 3"; Earrings, 1.25"). $18, $12.

A windmill design pin with faux marbled green stones on the blades. The clips on the earrings are marked Pat. Pend. (Pin, 2.25"; Earrings, 1" x .75"). $24, $16.

A golden stem holds a green enameled flower with a pearl center. (Pin, 2" x 1.5"; Earrings, 1.25" x 1"). $23, $15.

Avocado. "This classic circle pin takes on a new look and a rich one. Avocado green with a flash of darker olive through the center creates an interesting pattern of color in the slim oval stones nestled in the round. Matching button earrings, too."—*Emmons Showcase 1966.* (Pin, 1.5"; Earrings, 1"). $19, $12.

Victoria. The points of the dark green triangle are rounded and surrounded by a frame of golden bubbles. The matching earrings are trimmed in plain gold and hang 1.75" from a clip that gives the illusion of being for pierced ears. Pierced earrings not shown. 1971. (Pin, 2"; Earrings, .75" x 1.5"). $32, $20.

Colleen. These two golden chains can be taken apart and worn individually. The shorter of the two (18") has a removable bright green marbled oval pendant (4") with a tassel hanging from the end. The longer chain (30") has two green ovals along its length. The matching earrings are 1.25". Mid-1970s. $23, $15.

Queen of the Orient. Pendant and earrings of carved faux jade ovals surrounded by clear rhinestones. 1960. (Pendant and Earrings, 1"). $28, $18.

Mint Julep. Feathery, white enameled leaves accent golden ovals, each of which contains four tiny, pale mint green glass flowers with rhinestone centers. Necklace not shown. 1961. (Bracelet, 7"; Earrings, 1" x .75"). $22, $14.

Oracle. In antiqued gold-tone, a Mayan-like god with an elaborate filigree headdress. Eyes and other accents are jade green beads. Matching earrings not shown. 1973. (Pendant, 3"; Chain, 26"). $55.

Indian Summer. This strand of jade-colored beads is 29" long. The matching earrings are a simple loop of nine beads and hang down 2". One end of the beads is fastened to the front of the ear clip, the other end to the back of the clip. This allows the loop of beads to remain circular in shape when worn. Each bead on both the necklace and earrings is roughly .25" in diameter. In this collection, the beads also came in goldenrod, cinnamon, rust, and beige. 1976-78. $18, $12.

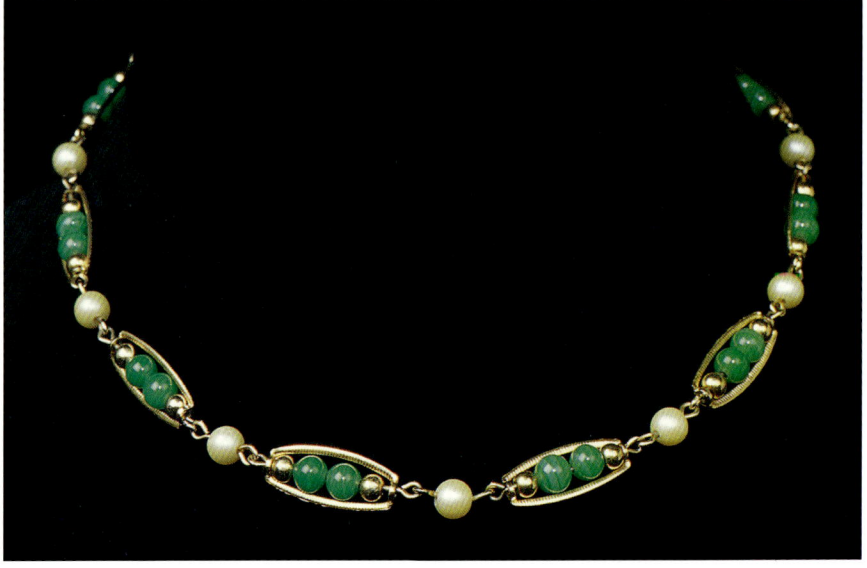

Limelight. "…light and breezy, with an Oriental feeling in its design. The soft, mint green blends beautifully with the pearly beads …"—*Emmons Showcase 1965*. Earrings not shown. (15"). $22.

Jade. This necklace with a tear drop of genuine jade in a gold-filled frame is from the Emmons Crown Collection. It was introduced with both pierced and clip earrings; a matching ring was added later. 1969-1974. (.5"). $24.

This silver-tone **Moppet** holding a faceted emerald ball is the birthstone necklace for May. Emmons offered children's jewelry as "Jewelry for Juniors." This is one of those pieces. 1974-79. (Pendant, 1"; Chain, 16"). $17.

A chartreuse enameled flower pin with a white button center. The yellow and coral versions are shown later in the book. Earrings not shown. (2.5"). $16.

Jelly Bean. Gold-tone pin with lime and chartreuse plastic pieces dates from 1969-70. Earrings not shown. (2"). $22.

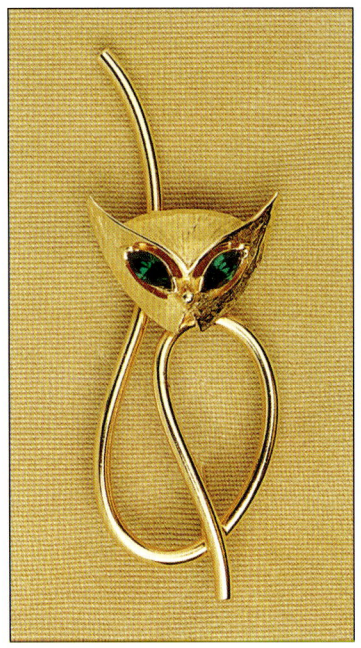

Glamour Puss. Gold wire swirled into the outline of a cat with emerald green rhinestone eyes. Mid-1960s. (2.5"). $24.

Salamander. This little gold fellow has green beads for his eyes and on his body. 1969. (2"). $24.

A faceted diamond shape of green glass hangs from a gold setting accented with a round topaz and citrine. (2.5"). $32.

Translucent avocado green rounds are held in their collar of small gold petals with filigree prongs. (1.25"). $20.

Red, Pink, and Purple

Thoughts of rubies, garnets, pink tourmalines, and amethysts might lead one to believe this category would be packed with spectacular rhinestone pieces. But, while many of the most extravagant of Emmons' rhinestone rings fit in this category, the rest consists of a potpourri of rhinestones, glass, plastic, and enamel with some interesting pieces from the fifties and early sixties.

A gold open-work four-leaf clover with a red glass center. Earrings not shown. (3.25" x 2.75"). $24.

Cherries Jubilee. Surrounded by a bold, golden setting, cherry red and black plastic dots circle a large cherry red cabochon. 1970. (Pin, 2" x 1.75"; Earrings, 1" x .75"). $24, $14.

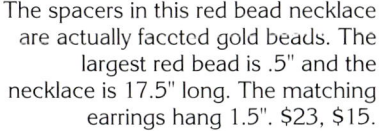

The spacers in this red bead necklace are actually faceted gold beads. The largest red bead is .5" and the necklace is 17.5" long. The matching earrings hang 1.5". $23, $15.

Crimson Glory. A stem of antiqued gold leaves serves as a surround for clear and aurora borealis pink rhinestones. Ruby red marquis-shaped rhinestones pop out among the pinks in these magnificent earrings. Pin not shown. Mid-1960s. (1.5" x 1.25"). $30.

Shiny silver flower earrings resemble pinwheels and have red aurora borealis rhinestone centers. (.75"). $22.

Based on a copyright description, we assume this is **Magic Wand**. The pale gold flower earrings have red aurora borealis rhinestone centers. The pin (not shown) is the same flower with a long, straight stem and is often referred to in online auctions as a sword. 1960. (1.5" x 1"). $22.

Cinnabar. Scrolled silver-tone backs hold bright red aurora borealis cabochons. Matching bracelet not shown. 1969. (1" x .75"). $22.

Golden Swirl. White button centers were designed to be snapped out of the settings and covered in fabric, as in our example showing red. Mid-1960s. (1.25"). $21.

Tuval Medallion. Red enameled disks with a scroll design hang from golden cones. Marked "EmJ." Pendant not shown. Mid-1950s. (1" disk; hanging length almost 2"). $21.

This little lizard has a faux marcasite body with red rhinestone markings and eyes. He is slightly larger than his cousin, **Salamander** (see p. 92). (2.5"). $24.

Crimson Rose. Fourteen prong-set, red rhinestones sit on a gold filigree base. 1971-72. (1"). $23.

The gold filigree band looks like **Spring Reverie** from the early 1970s; however, the stone is a clear red oval instead of a green oval. Perhaps someone replaced the original stone. $20.

Caroline Birthstone Ring. Garnet. This style of birthstone ring was introduced in 1972 and continued through 1977. $26.

Lotus Flower. Golden rays swirl out from under the just-opening blossom of a delicate pink lotus flower. Mid-1960s. (Pin, 2.25"; Earrings, 1.25"). $23, $15.

Fashion Tracery. The pink and gold version of these lacy flowers. Early 1970s. (Pin, 2.5"; Earrings, 1.25"). $22, $15.

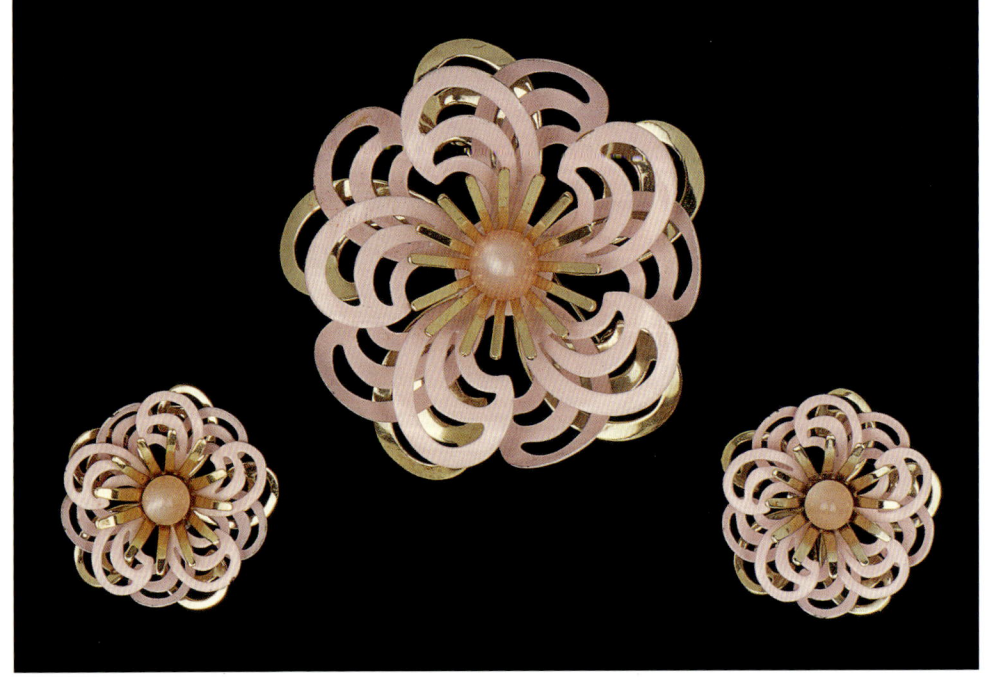

Flutter. This enameled butterfly with orange and gold highlights was available from 1968 to 1974. (2" x 1.5"). $21.

Apostrophe-shaped earrings in bright yellow. Matching bracelet not shown. (1.25"). $14.

More apostrophes, this time in bright orange. The matching orange hinged bangle bracelet is 2.5" in diameter. Also came in powder blue and sage green. $21, $14.

Butterscotch. Bracelet made of four smooth butterscotch-colored rectangular stones set in brushed gold. 1978. (6"). $21.

Parfait Bib. Another clunky, fun necklace, this time in sunny yellows. Earrings not shown. (17"). $23.

The chains of these drop earrings end in coral beads. (2.25"). $17.

Tutti-Frutti (incomplete). We have two pieces in yellow of the Tutti-Frutti collection—a necklace of plastic ovals faceted to make them glimmer, and a swirling silver-tone pin with long teardrop-shaped yellow cabochons. The necklace originally came with a plain silver chain. The necklace, pin, and earrings (not shown) were introduced in the spring of 1972 and also came in white and lavender. In the catalog published that fall, only the necklaces remained. Turquoise and green necklaces were added in the spring of 1973. (Necklace, 36"; Pin, 2.25"). $15, $23.

Indian Summer. This time we have the goldenrod beads. See p. 90 for a full description of this collection. $18, $12.

Dawning Glory. Large, fluted coral domes are surrounded with pearls and set in a corona of bright golden flames. This set is very heavy. 1970. (Pin, 2" x 1.75; Earrings, 1" x 1.5"). $28, $17.

Two rows of coral beads surround a center pearl and are set among golden beads that are actually the prongs. (1.5"). $21.

Dawning Glory ring. (1.5" x 1"). $32.

Carved coral flowers set in simple, pale gold frames. The choker is only 11.5" long, so we think it was created from two bracelets. (Bracelet, 6.5"; Earrings, .75"). $17, $10, $7.

113

A bright orange rhinestone sits on top of two rows of deeper orange navettes that glow like the embers of a fire. All the stones are prong set. Earrings and ring not shown. The pin is 2" in diameter and .75" high. $35.

Regal Splendor. Bright orange and green rhinestones in an antiqued gold-tone filigree setting. The drop portion of the earrings was also available as a clip earring (not shown). Early 1970s. (Pin, 2.25"; Drop Earrings, 2"). $26, $16.

The high setting (.5") hides the fact that the stone spins to show turquoise on one side (p. 85) and coral on the other. $32.

Budding Romance. Lovely gold open-work settings with orange and yellow rhinestones. 1969. (Pin, 2.25"; Earrings, 1"). $24, $16.

Antique Star. Delicate antiqued gold star with coral and pearls. Marked "Caroline." 1974. (1"). $24.

Coralette. This ring goes quite nicely with **African Queen** on p. 120. Marked "Caroline." 1975-1976. (1" x .75"). $22.

Multi-colored and Miscellaneous

While some of the pieces in this grouping defy categorization, e.g., lustrous gold-speckled copper-colored plastic, we certainly cannot consider them as residual or leftovers. Shimmering rainbows of rhinestones, exotic cultures, and the patriotic "red, white, and blue" are just a few of the themes present in this assortment of pieces.

Set under arches of gold, faceted ovals of coppery goldstones paired with aurora borealis rhinestones bring a lot of sparkle to this set. (Necklace, 15"; Bracelet, 7.5"; Earrings, 1.25"). $23, $18, $15.

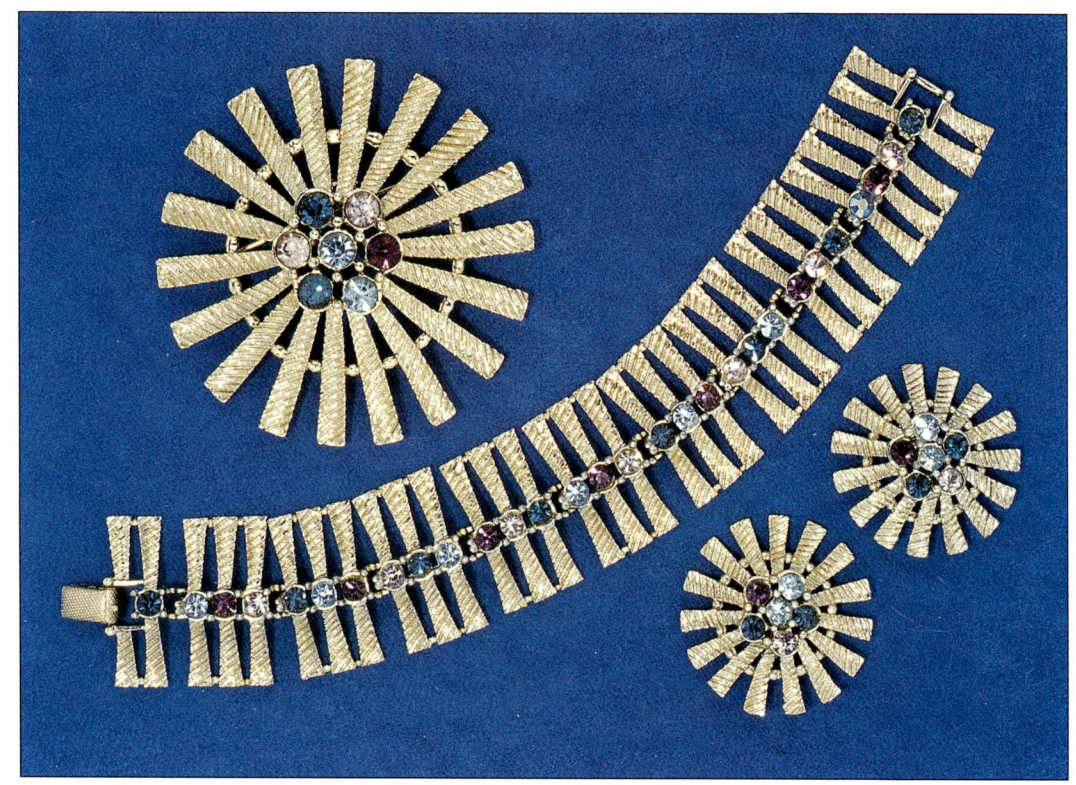

In this striking pin, grooved ribs curve upward over a golden ring to hold a cluster of mauve, blue, and purple rhinestones. (Pin, 2.75"; Bracelet, 7.5"; Earrings, 1.75"). $38, $23, $20.

A grid of mixed pastel aurora borealis round rhinestones fills the center of a silver rope circle. (Pin, 2.25"; Earrings, 1.5"). $35, $24.

Floral Antique. Small flowers with orange, blue, pink, and green rhinestone centers are captured in ovals of antiqued gold ropes. The bracelet is a hinged bangle. 1975-1977. Earrings not shown. (Pendant, 1" x .5"; Bracelet, 2.5" dia.; Ring, 1" x .5"). $19, $26, $21.

Cleopatra. As the name implies, this set is fit for a queen. The antiqued gold rectangles have embossed geometric designs and are studded with topaz-, peridot-, and amethyst-colored rhinestones. 1976-77. (Necklace, 28"; Pendant, 3.5"; Bracelet, 7.25"; Earrings, 1" with a .5" drop). $38, $23, $15.

Thick, shiny loops studded with multicolored rhinestones. The loops swing from an inverted teardrop. Pendant and earrings are the same size. (1.5" x .75"). $15, $23.

A necklace of colorful hearts framed in gold. The earrings are clear fuchsia hearts framed in gold and suspended from a lavender stud. They are marked "EmJ." See a copy of an ad featuring this necklace on p. 15. 1959. (Necklace, 16"; Earrings, just over 1"). $21, $14.

Miniature gardens of seed pearl flowers, multi-colored aurora borealis rhinestones, and clear pink and gray cabochons are set in etched silver squares. The heavy silver chain is permanently attached to a split fleur-de-lis set with a red aurora borealis rhinestone at the top of the pendant. (Pendant, 1.5" x 1"; Earrings, 1"). $22, $15.

Garden Bouquet. Tiny white plastic flowers with pastel rhinestone centers bloom on delicate golden stems. Matching earrings are the same size as the pin. 1959. (Pin and Earrings, 2.25"). $18, $27.

Eternal Spring. A matte gold feather pin is adorned with a spray of golden leaves and delicate white plastic flowers with pastel aurora borealis centers. Early 1960s. (Pin, 2.25" x 1.25"; Earrings, 2" x 1.25"). $20, $28.

A garland of white enameled flowers with pastel rhinestone centers, this silver-tone necklace is marked with the Emmons crown tag. The adjustable length goes from choker to 16". Bracelet and earrings not shown. $32.

Nostalgia. The centerpieces of this set are black ovals with delicate red and yellow roses and blue forget-me-nots. The ovals in the choker and bracelet are framed by heavy, silver-tone chain. The bracelet is a wide, hinged bangle of embossed silver-tone metal. The choker is marked with a round Emmons tag. Mid-1970s. (Choker, 14"; Bracelet, 2.25" dia.). $12, $17. Ring, $11.

Kaleidoscope. On this open-work pin, small plastic pieces in a variety of shapes, sizes, and colors are sprinkled among tiny clear rhinestones. Mid-1960s. (Pin, 2"; Earrings, .75"). $24, $16.

Persian Treasure. In the center of an elaborate, antiqued gold open-work setting are three coral-colored navettes. The piece is further decorated with bright aqua aurora borealis rhinestones. Early 1960s. (Pin, 3"; Earrings, 1.25"). $37, $25.

African Queen. Coral, emerald green, and golden topaz stones are shown to their best advantage in an antiqued gold setting. Mid-1970s. (Bracelet, 7.5"; Pin/Pendant, 2.5"; Earrings, 1"). $25, $15, $10.

Legacy. Regal purple and bright green baguettes cover the brim of hat-shaped, antiqued gold disks. These disks alternate with gold rectangles set with deep purple stones surrounded by tiny gold disks. This was a Royal Hostess gift in 1971-72. (Bracelet, 6.5"; Earrings, .75"). $25, $17.

Legacy ring. $25.

Framed in golden laurels, these large cabochons in green, coral, black, and blue are flecked with gold. The matching earrings came in several different colors; blue and coral are shown. (Bracelet, 6.5"; Earrings, 1.25"). $19, $12.

Moonglo. "Soft, lustrous colors of moonstones are styled in a lacy, golden setting. A rainbow of hues to blend with all costumes."—*Emmons Showcase 1966*. The earrings shown here are in goldenrod; they also came in a soft rose hue. (Bracelet, 7.25"; Earrings, 1" x .75"). $16, $10.

Collection of bracelets. Top to bottom: **Scimitar**. This is today's slide bracelet-look in a piece from the 1970s. Half moons and other shapes in Florentine gold are encrusted with jewels and separated by pearls. $23. A scarab bracelet, so popular in the 1950s, has blue, green, pink, and turquoise scarabs separated by single pearls wrapped in gold wire and is marked "EmJ" on a hang tag, with the copyright symbol on the reverse side of the tag. $26. **Arabesque**. "The heirloom look of finely crafted Jewelry is seen in this exotic Bracelet in a handsome Florentine finish. It has intricate design and multi-faceted charm that will fascinate all who gaze at the wrist that wears Emmons. Arabesque. Color, appeal and a look of intrigue…and there's something else, too! When you want a different look, wear it in reverse and each exciting link becomes a studied treasure in antique allure."—*Emmons Showcase 1965*. $26. (All, 7.5").

Antique Swirl. A 1" diameter pendant in antiqued gold set with amethyst, turquoise, and a pearl in the center. 1973. $21.

Medallia. A variety of colored beads are set in a 2.25" Florentine gold corona charm that is attached to a 34" gold chain. Could be worn either as a necklace or a belt. 1969. $37.

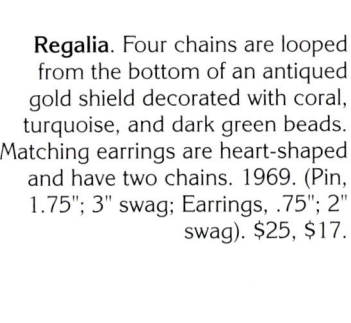

Antigua. Faux pearls, turquoise beads, and amethysts sit on each side of a large amethyst rhinestone. 1972. (3"). $22.

Regalia. Four chains are looped from the bottom of an antiqued gold shield decorated with coral, turquoise, and dark green beads. Matching earrings are heart-shaped and have two chains. 1969. (Pin, 1.75"; 3" swag; Earrings, .75"; 2" swag). $25, $17.

These three necklaces were available in juicy lime, lemon, and orange colors with fluted gold spacers. (18"). $12 ea.

Candyland. A lightweight gold chain with four sets of five small rounds in marbled green, rose, blue, turquoise, and coral. It is 60" long and can be separated into 15" and 45" lengths. Earrings not shown. 1974-75. $28.

Pretty Pastel. The flowers etched in the frosted blue, green, and pink cubes are washed in white. Marked with a round tag stamped "Emmons" on the back. Earrings not shown. 1975. (14"). $18.

Mardi Gras. A choker of plastic beads in colors of the tropics—flamingo pink, lemon yellow, and lime green. 1961. (16"). $27.

A necklace of yellow and orchid bell-like flowers accented with clear rhinestones. The original card shows item number 3598. (14"). $21.

Autumn colors in marquis- and round-shaped glass stones are accented with tiny hot pink rhinestones along the outer edge of this circle pin. One stone is missing. (2"). $32.

Twinkling Butterfly. The outline of a golden butterfly is decorated with multicolored aurora borealis rhinestones; the head and the ends of the antennae are pearls. Early 1960s. (2.25" x 1.25"). $24.

In gold-tone it's called **Calypso**. We have not found any documentation for this silvery version. The rough surface of the oval is set with six rhinestones in aqua, two ruby, amethyst, emerald and golden topaz. (1.5" x 1"). $22.

This small crown appears to be washed in pale gold and set with rhinestones in ruby, emerald, and sapphire. We have not been able to discover the significance, if any, of the initials "H C F" in raised script on the front of the crown. (1"). $16.

Jeweled Dragonfly. Clear aurora borealis rhinestones make his body and wings sparkle. Add a red rhinestone baguette at his neck and two emerald rhinestone eyes, and he's as "cute as a bug in rug!" 1966. (2"). $24.

Crown Royale. A gold crown with three large cabochons in jewel-tone red, green, and blue is further decorated with clear rhinestones and pearls. Christmas 1972. (2" x 1.5"). $23.

Raggedy Ann. She's a golden pendant version of, according to the *Emmons Showcase 1965*, "the best-loved of all dolls." (1.5"). $24.

Left: Pendant in silver-tone, possibly a stylized pinecone, is decorated with red rhinestones with more stones in the scalloped gold border. Date unknown. Right: **Candlelight**. Candle-shaped pin with red and blue rhinestones. 1968. (Pendant, 2.75" x 1.75"; Pin, 2"). $24, $24.

Available from 1971 to 1979, **Cloisonne Necklace** was a piece in a collection of jewelry for children, "Junior Jewelry for your little doll."— *Caroline Emmons Showcase Spring and Summer 1971*. Matching bracelet and ring not shown. (.5"). $12.

Enameled flowers of red with green leaves accented by two pearls on this charm have an Oriental look. (1"). $22.

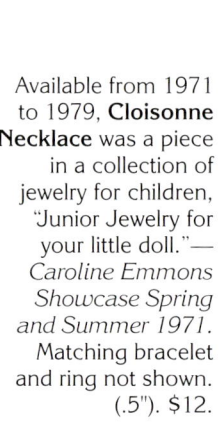

Fan in closed position.

Dainty, gold fan pendant (open). The fan hangs 2.25" when closed. When opened to its full 2" width, an enameled red and blue bird flying through white clouds is displayed. $24.

Charmettes. "...a lovable bracelet that is bright, gay and devastatingly graceful."—*Emmons Showcase 1965.* Charms of red, blue, and yellow glass alternate with .5" gold disks. (7"). $27.

Americana. A circle formed of pointed silver swirls, the inner sides of which are enameled in red, white, and blue. Matching earrings are a section of the circle. This is the 1970 set. A different set with the same name was sold in 1975. (Pin, 1.5"; Earrings, 1"). $17, $11.

Starburst. This set of patriotic red, white, and blue cabochons in gold-tone is ready for the 4th of July! Pierced earrings not shown. 1971-72. (Pin, 2.75"; Earrings, 1.25"). $24, $10.

Spirit of '76. Patriotic red, white, and blue enameling on the 2" silver pendant says it all! The chain is 24", but it can be adjusted for shorter lengths. It was available in the spring of 1976 through summer of 1977. *Courtesy of Dawn Levickas.* $34.

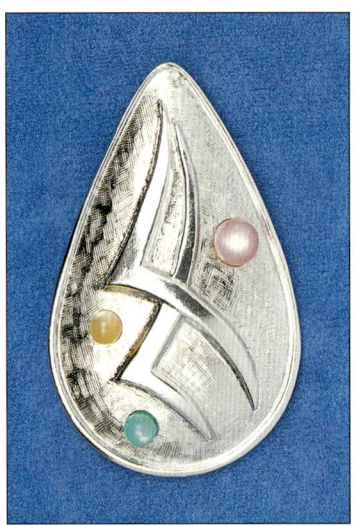

A brushed silver-tone pendant accented with a polished, free-form design in the center and three cat's-eye beads to catch the light. (2.75" x 1.75"). $22.

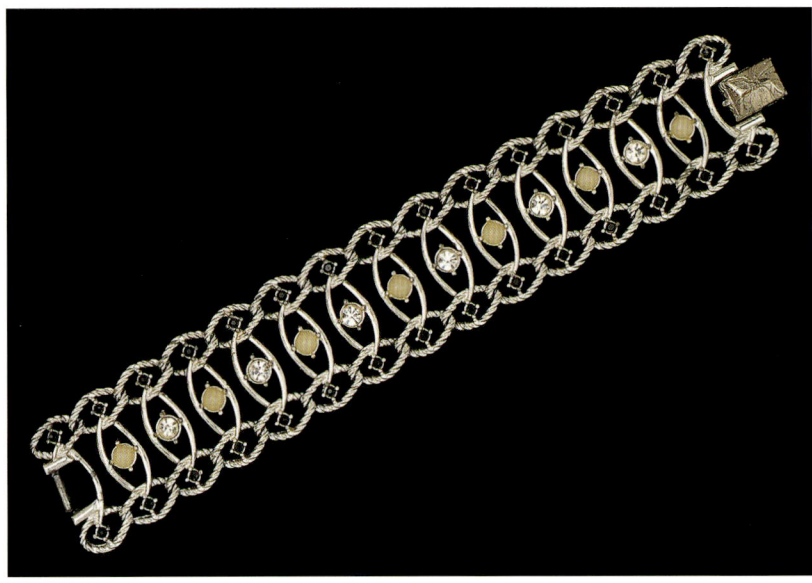

Loops of silver rope are threaded through smooth silver ovals and joined together to form the edges of this 7" bracelet. The center of each oval is set with pearls and clear rhinestones (alternating). There are tiny, faceted black beads at either end of each oval. (7" x 1.25"). $22.

Galaxy. Simulated jewels adorn a modernistic silver star in one of the larger Emmons pieces. Mid-1960s. (4" x 2"). $40.

A ribbon of gold so pale it is sometimes mistaken for silver-tone wraps around three fruit-salad style cabochons in aurora borealis colors. The ribbon is studded with six clear rhinestones. Matching earrings not shown. (2.5" x 1"). $24.

This round, silver-tone pin with a black-glass center is surrounded by clear aurora borealis rhinestones that form a star. Five navettes in taupe form another star shape, and all are accented with tiny black-glass stones. Earrings not shown. (2.5"). $34.

A gold-tone bar pin with a clear center cabochon and simulated pearls at the ends. When you look into the cabochon there is a stained glass effect created by tiny pieces of brightly colored foil under the cabochon. (3.5"). $17.

Nefertiti. Look through the clear cabochons to find profiles of the Egyptian queen in black and gold on mother-of-pearl. Frames are a scalloped edge of gold. Necklace, bracelet, cufflinks, and tie bar not shown. Marked "EmJ." 1950s. (1"). $16.

Spring Fever. The gold chain extends the 2" white plastic arc with colorful stripes into a necklace 17" long. 1979. $16.

Milky Way. A scalloped, oval-shaped pendant in brushed gold set with nineteen opalescent rhinestones. (1"). Earrings are round with seven stones. Matching ring and drop pierced earrings not shown. 1969-71. $23, $15.

Jeweled Charm. A lovely gold chain bracelet with a round charm covered in stones that are wired in place. As an Emmons Crown Collection piece, the stones are semi-precious—a cultured pearl surrounded by Wyoming jade, adventurine, sodolite, and rose quartz; the bracelet is 1/20 12K gold filled. 1964. $24.

Moonglow. Opalescent glass teardrop pendant on a gold chain. (Pendant, 1" including bale; Chain, 16"). Late 1970s. $18.

This piece is similar in style to **Fortune Teller**. The *Emmons Showcase 1966* describes the cabochons in the charm on that bracelet as having a "…veritable rainbow of color…," and the picture shows two pinkish stones. Our bracelet has one pink cabochon and one in hematite. We don't know if this is an earlier or later version, an individual's customization, or a different piece entirely. (Chain, 7.5"; Charm, .75" x .5" x .5"). $18.

Midnight Lace (incomplete). The large opal cabochon is surrounded by eight faceted opals set in a black filigree frame. The matching black chain is missing. Earrings not shown. 1969-81. (Pin/Pendant, 2.75" x 2.5"). $23.

Mother's Pin. The center of this gold-tone heart pin is offset and holds tiny rhinestones signifying the birth month of children or grandchildren. The pin in the upper left has three stones with the remaining spaces filled with seed pearls; in the lower right, all eight spaces are filled with colorful stones. 1969-1981. (1.5" x 1.25"). $24.

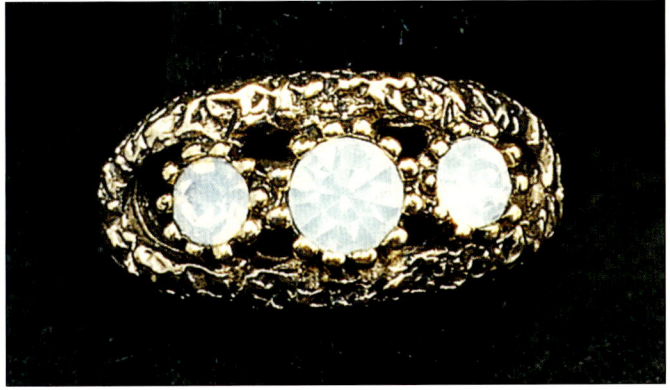

Moonbeams. Faceted opals set in antiqued gold. 1974-75. (.5" wide). $23.

Broad, polished silver-tone petals cup to hold multicolored rhinestones, some with an aurora borealis coating, in these bold, yet lightweight flower earrings. Some rhinestones are missing. (1.5"). $28.

Clear plastic dome earrings are etched on the bottom to pick up a kaleidoscope of color. They are set in a plain gold frame. (.75"). $19.

Collection of rings. Left to right: **White Classic**. Rounded ends on .75" stone that sits on three gold bands. 1977-78. $18. **Betsy Ross**. Tiny faceted beads in red, white, and blue sit on the ends of a wrap-around silver rope ring. 1975-77. $18. **Tapestry**. The white oval was stamped with a grid pattern, making the painted flowers look as though they were done in needlepoint. 1975. $14.

Gold petals with white enameled centers offer up a large aurora borealis rhinestone. Pin not shown. (2"). $27.

Granada. Multicolored rhinestones set in antiqued silver swirls. 1972-73. (Ring, 1"). $22.

Free-form golden twigs grasp a variety of stones—marbleized beads, a pearl, clear cabochons, and aurora borealis blue rhinestones. (Ring, 1"). $27.

Just Silver

Not until the 1970s were many designs offered in both silver- and gold-tone. In 1965, there were twenty-one designs, about one-quarter of the total women's collection, that were just gold- or silver-tone, i.e., without any form of stone or color decoration. Of these twenty-one, one was a combination of gold- and silver-tone. Only two designs were offered in a choice of silver or gold—**Gleaming Bows** and **Circle Twist**. Of those offered in either silver- or gold-tone, about 60 percent were gold-tone and 40 percent silver-tone. In 1970, there were only seventeen metal-only designs, but almost 65 percent of them were offered in a choice of silver- or gold-tone and 30 percent in only gold-tone. Just one pair of earrings, **Saucy Squares**, was offered only in silver-tone. This leads us to believe that the number of just silver-tone designs could be significantly less than the number of just gold-tone designs.

Crescent-shaped lattices of tiny silver beads connected to swirls of dimpled silver. The 14"-16" necklace is marked with the Emmons crown tag. The bracelet of double crescents is 7", and the earrings are 1.75" x .75". The item number for the earrings is 2769. 1960. $26, $16, $10.

Disks, disks, and more disks! The necklace has a double row of silver disks with alternating polished and textured finishes. The bracelet is a triple row, and the earrings are single shiny disks with a large surround of textured silver. (Necklace, 14"; Bracelet, 6.25"; Earrings, 1"). $29, $17, $11.

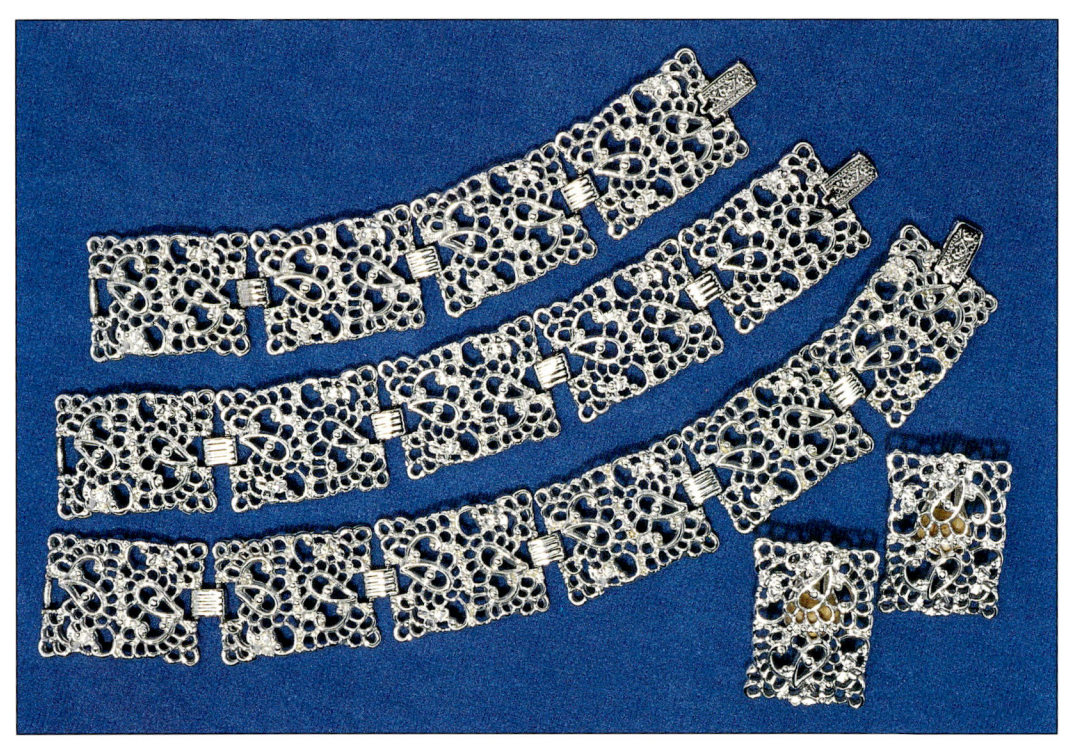

These lacy silver rectangles come in six-link (8"), five-link (7") and four-link (5.5") lengths. We have no documentation on these pieces so can only speculate as to what was intended. Do we have three bracelets? Or perhaps two meant to be linked to form a choker? The matching earrings are the same size as the individual links—1.25" x 1". $18, $16, $14.

Brocade. Silver ropes outline the sections of this bracelet, and each section is filled with lacy little flowers. Matching earrings are ovals made in the same way. Mid-1960s. (Bracelet, 6.5" x 1"; Earrings, 1" x .75"). $20, $14.

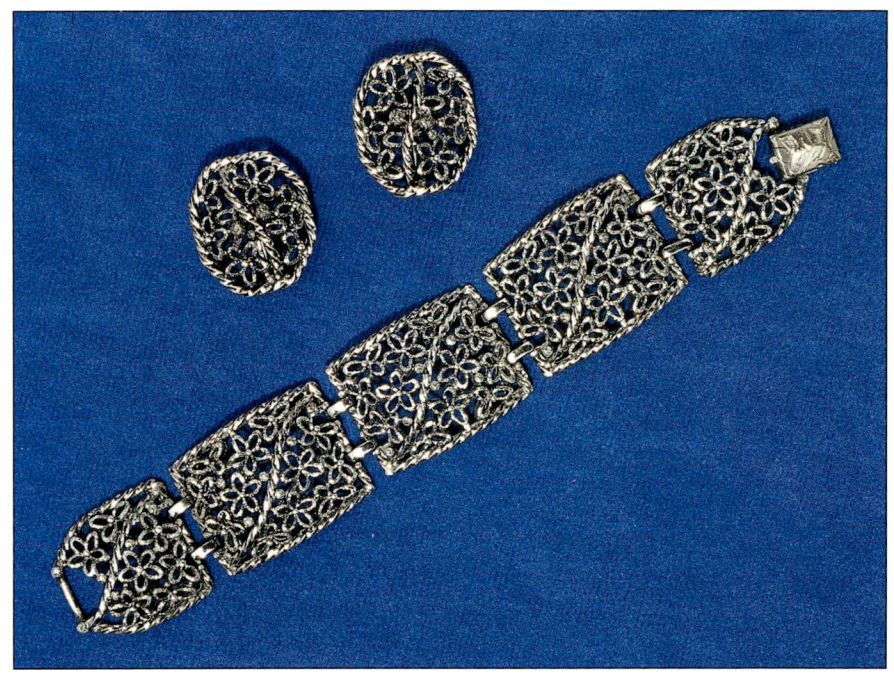

Although it looks heavy, this silver-tone choker and bracelet with etched pillow-like clip fasteners is very lightweight. It is marked "EmJ." Matching earrings in gold-tone are shown on p. 172. (Choker, 13"; Bracelet, 7"). $15, $11.

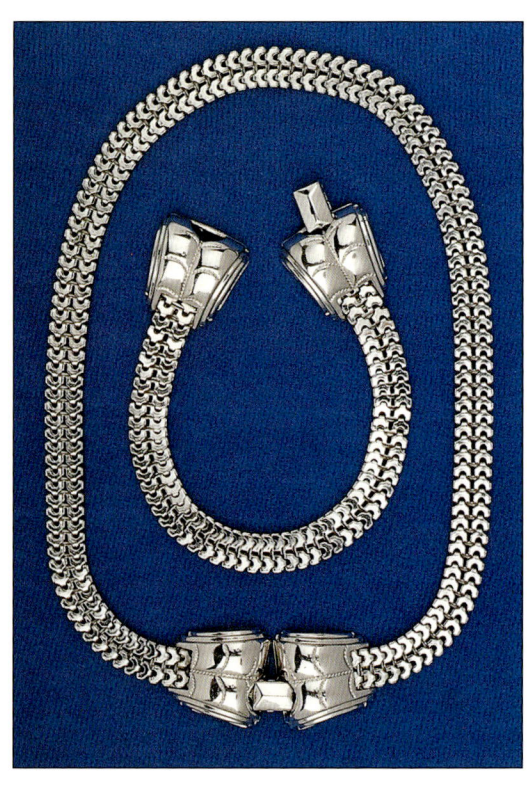

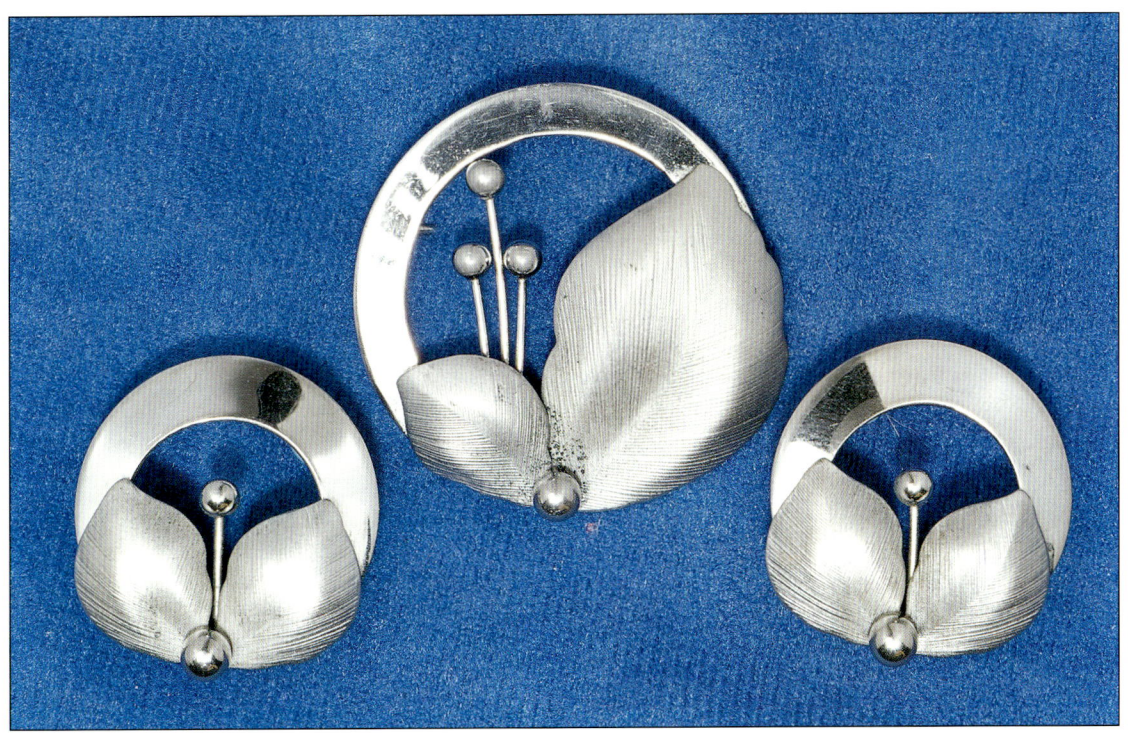

Hi-Fashion. Art-deco style circle pin of a stylized flower. 1959. (Pin, 1.75"; Earrings, 1"). $21, $15.

Sculptura. Antiqued silver-tone pin with embossed flowers on the surface. Matching ears are arcs cut from the larger circle, and the ends are scalloped. Early 1970s. (Pin, 1.5"; Earrings, 1"). $20, $13.

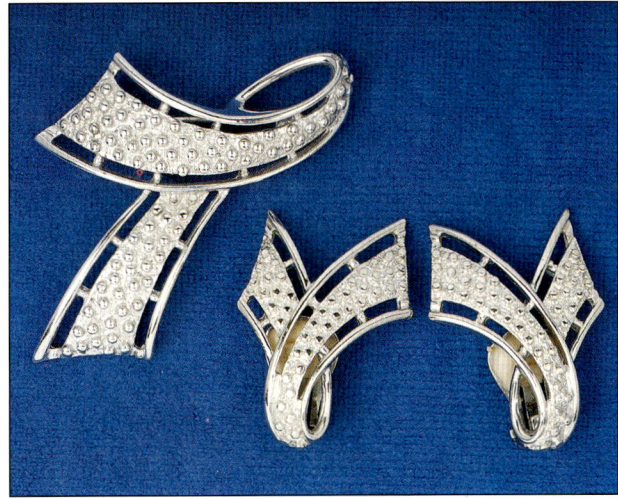

Spectator. A nubby ribbon of silver that, according to the *Emmons Showcase 1965*, has a "sleek bow knot design." It is designed to be worn with the ends of the ribbon pointing up. (Pin, 2.5"; Earrings, 1.5"). $18, $12.

Sonnet. "…tailored beauty that is rich in design and texture…"—*Emmons Showcase 1965*. A wide, curving band covered with leafy fronds in relief. Mid-1960s. (Pin, 2"; Earrings, 1"). $22, $14.

Two bright silver feathers overlap, and the fine detailing is accented with a light, white wash. (Pin, 3.25" x .5"; Earrings, 1.25" x .5"). $17, $11.

Luster Leaf. These highly polished silver maple leaves have slits in the center of each lobe and are an early set. The earrings have screw-backs. Mid-1950s. (Pin, 2.5" x 2"; Earrings, 1"). $16, $10.

Silhouette. The large silver-tone form of a leaf has three smaller solid leaves in its center. Earrings match the solid leaves. 1961. (Pin, 2.5" x 2.25"; Earrings, 1.5"). $17, $11.

The gold-tone set is called **Golden Fern** (p. 156). Is this Silvery Fern? 1960s. (Pin, 3"; Earrings, 1.5" x 1"). $16, $11.

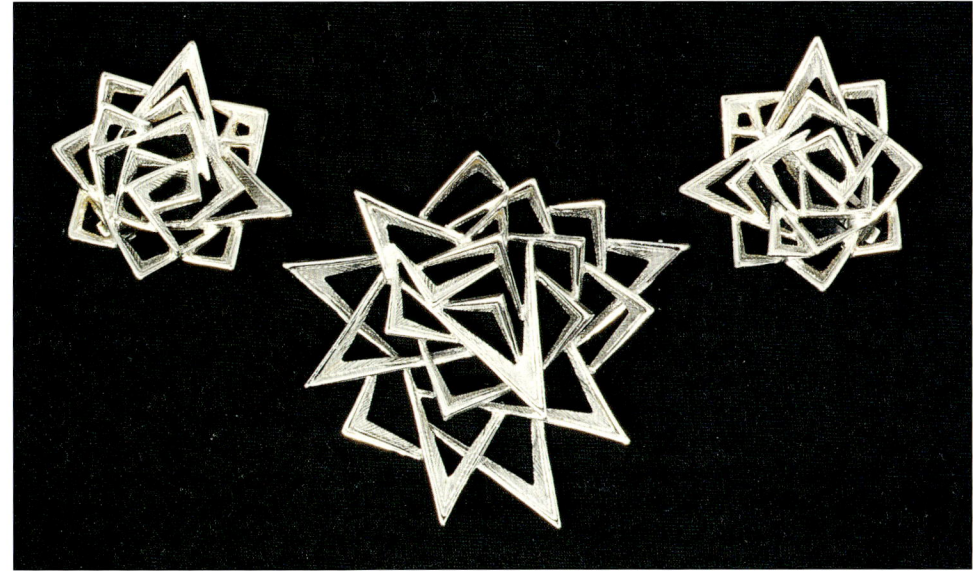

Beauty Points. A collection of brushed silver points outlined in polished silver. Mid-1960s. (Pin, 2.5"; Earrings, 1.5"). $22, $15.

Stem of six bright, brushed-silver leaves. Matching earrings have two leaves, their stems curled at the base. (Pin, 4"; Earrings, 1.75"). $26, $18.

This pendant is a ribbon of multi-textured silver patches. Three eyelets have been cut out in the widest portion. (Pendant, 2"; Earrings, 1.25"). $15, $10.

Silver-tone filigree flower with a fluted center (some discoloration) and silver ball stamens (3.5"). Matching filigree earrings resemble the profile of a tulip. (1.75" x 1.5"). $26, $18.

Delicate Spiral. Pendant and pierced earrings of thin silver wire spiral into concentric circles. The upper circles on the pendant are fixed; the lower swings from the other two. Cuff bracelet not shown. 1975-77. (Pendant, 3"; Earrings, 1.5"). $17, $7.

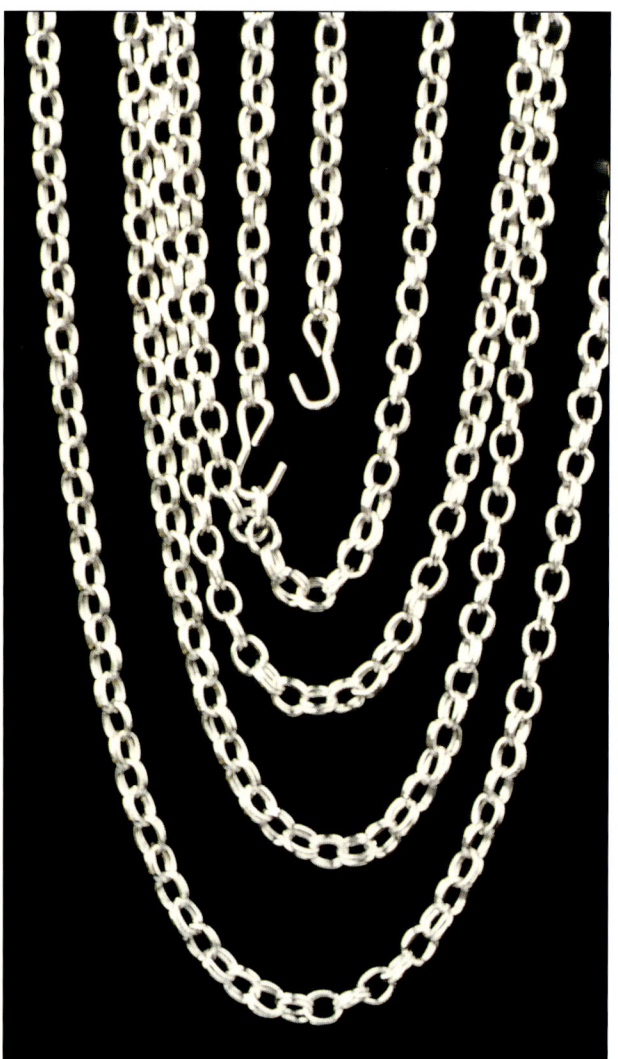

Endless Fashion. In the 1970 Christmas *Showcase*, this 100-inch chain is billed as the "Chain of Fashion Magic." It is shown as a multi-strand necklace, a *sautoir* belt, and body jewelry. $26.

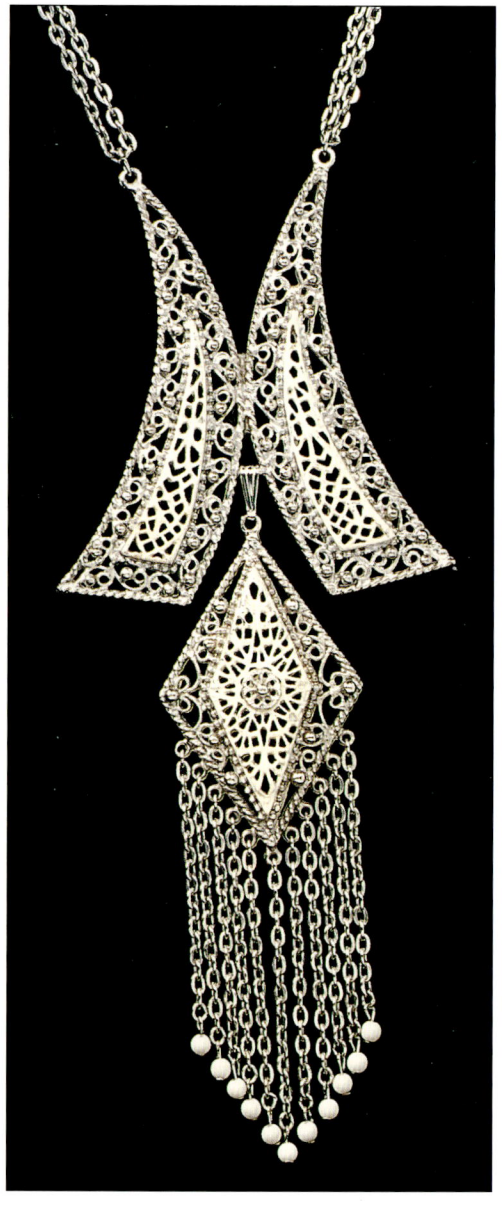

Arabian Nights. A stunning hostess gift, this articulated necklace is made of heavy silver-tone filigree that is enameled in ivory in the center of each section. A double chain is attached to the each side of the 7" pendant. The total length is 15". 1973-75. $53.

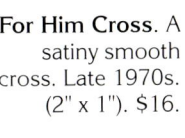

For Him Cross. A satiny smooth cross. Late 1970s. (2" x 1"). $16.

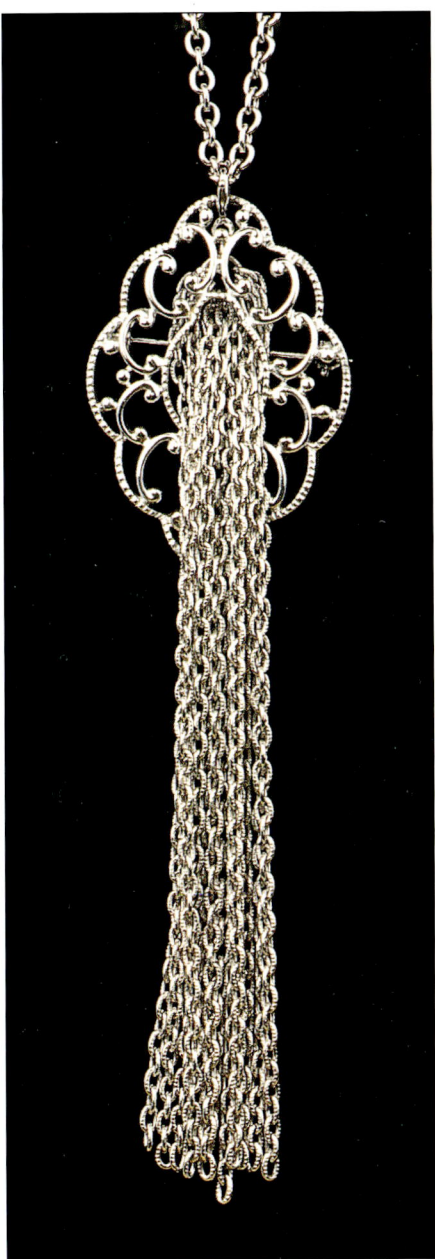

Show Off. This is a bright silver 3-piece set, and the chain, the pin/pendant, and the tassel can be worn together or separately. *Courtesy of Dawn Levickas.* Earrings not shown. Also came in gold-tone (not shown). 1972-74. (Chain, 24"; Pin/Pendant, 2.25" x 1.75"; Tassel, 6"). $16, $18, $10.

From at least the early 1960s, Emmons included at least one cross in each of its catalogs. The same was not true for Sarah Coventry. However, in 1973, Sarah Coventry began introducing a Limited Edition cross each year. Sarah Coventry's **Today** cross from the mid-1970s is shown on the left with Emmons' **Regency** cross on the right. (3" x 2.25"). $23 ea.

Three pendants in silver-tone. Left to right: **Serenity**, **Shining Faith** (also came in gold-tone with matching earrings), **Everlasting** (for gold, see p. 163). (Chains, 14"-16"; Pendants, .75"-1.25"). *Courtesy of Dawn Levickas.* $18 ea.

Three fine silver chains. Left to right: **Little Something** is 14.5". Also came in a 20" length and in gold-tone. 1975-78. $18. **Guys & Dolls** is a 19" barley corn chain. The gold version of this is shown on p. 163. 1980s. $18. **Identity**. These initial pendants came in A-Z in silvery finish only. 1978-80. (Chain, 17"; "X," .75"). $20.

Mask of comedy pendant in shiny silver-tone. (1"). $14.

Rose Lace. Filigree silver roses are set along the delicate chain. 1980. (15"-17"). *Courtesy of Dawn Levickas.* $22.

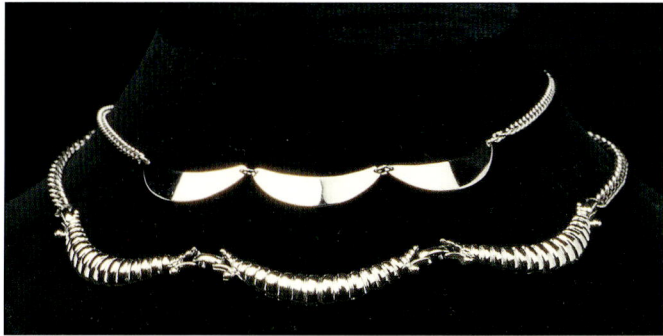

Two silver chokers. Top: **Moon Love**, polished silver crescent moons are strung together in this late 1970s necklace. (16"). $16. Bottom: A more elaborate take on this simple design with crescents that are deeply grooved in a spiral design with tiny silver beads at each end of the crescents. (12"). $18.

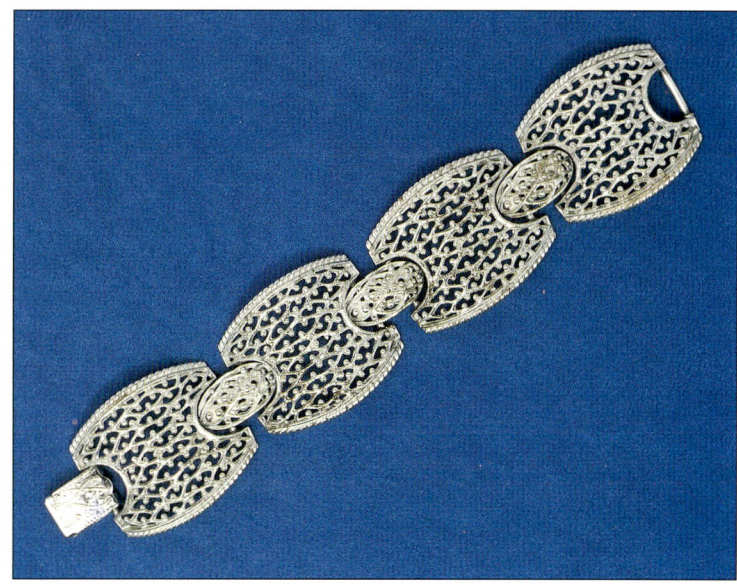

Fashion Frost. Tiny beads of silver accent the delicate filigree work keeping this substantial bracelet entirely feminine. Earrings not shown. 1962. (7" x 1.25"). $24.

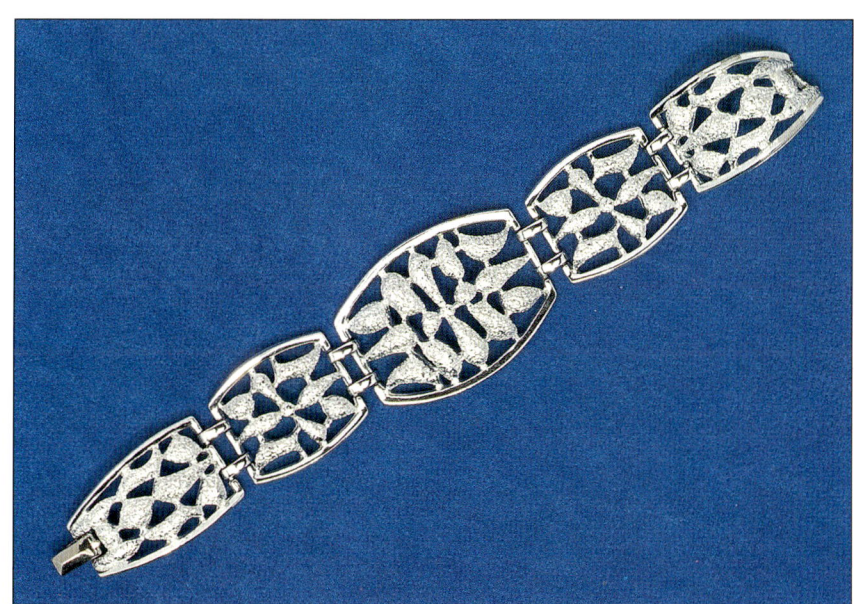

Frosty Lace. A bracelet of five open-work sections in flocked silver. The gold version of this bracelet is shown on p. 165. 1971-72. (7"). $18.

Cuff 'n Collar (incomplete). This looks as though someone has done a loose crochet of silver wire. The bracelet came with an extender (missing) to turn it into a choker. The gold version is shown on p. 165. 1971-73. (6.5"). $17.

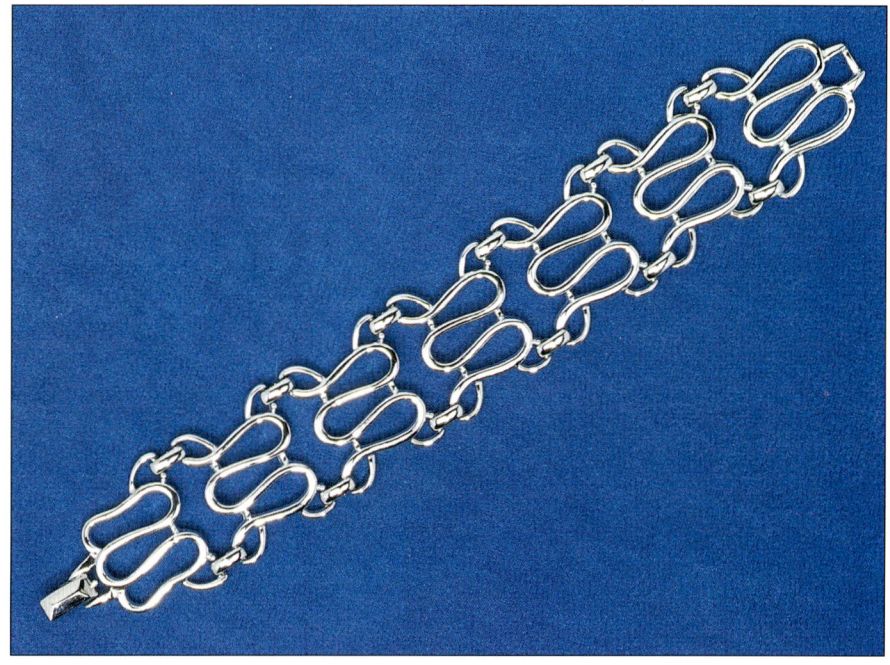

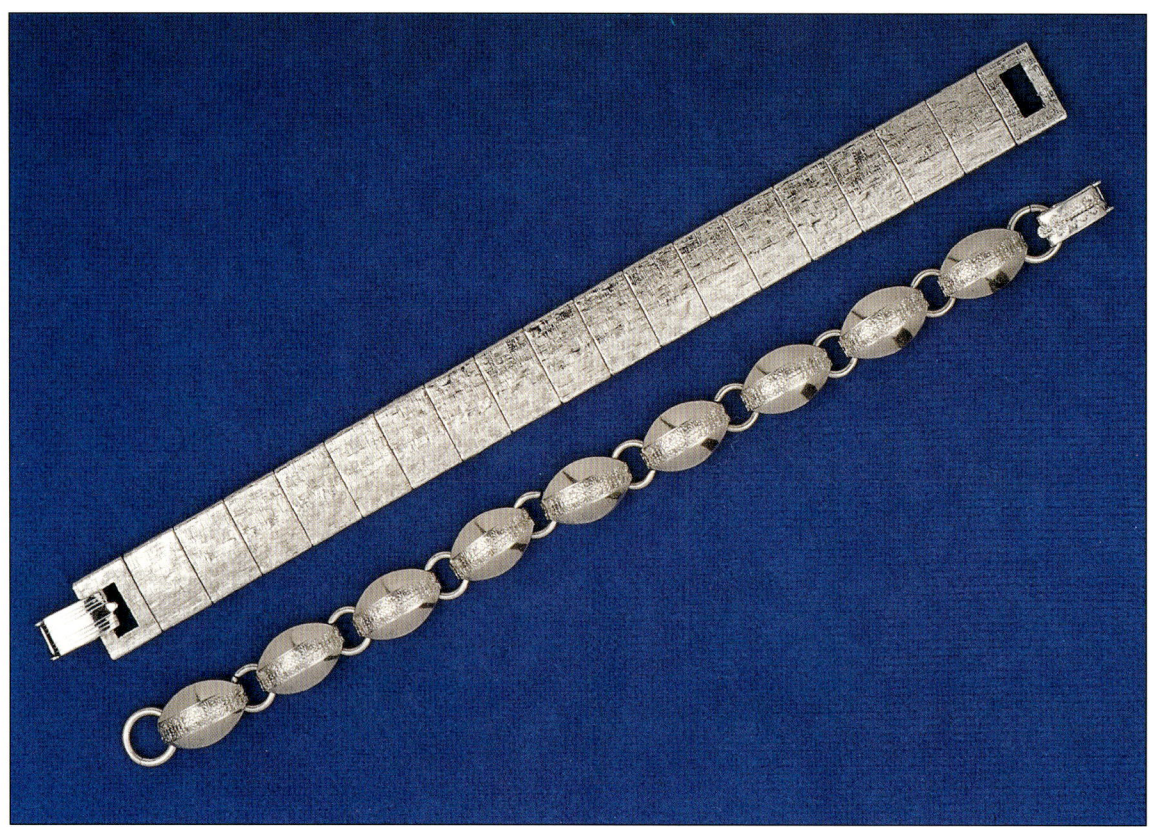

Two silver bracelets. Top: **Times Square**, a silver mesh bracelet encased in solid brushed silver rectangles. The gold version was introduced in 1974 (see p. 166). Silver was added in 1975, and both were available until 1981. (6.75"). $15. Bottom: concave silver ovals have a delicate design stamped across their tops. (7"). $14.

Flair. A hinged bangle in brushed silver. 1976-78. (2.5"). $19.

Silver bracelets. Left to right: **Reflection**, a bangle polished to a mirror-like finish from 1978-79, $12; **Quartet**, four bangles in a variety of finishes held together by a silver loop, 1969-76, $18; a narrow embossed bangle, $12; and **Open Road**, two "lanes" of silver separate on the back of the wrist, 1978, $12.

A satin-finished cuff with a darkened scroll design. $19.

Zodiac Charm. In this photo, the original packaging of rich simulated red leather decorated with a gold leaf "E," signifies that this Libra charm is part of the Emmons' Crown Collection of semi-precious jewelry. It is hand-brocaded (meaning a raised design done by hand) on sterling silver. 1960s. (.75"). $24.

Two silver bracelets. Left to right: **Roundabout** is hinged and came with matching earrings, 1969-71, $16; **Embraceable** is also hinged and has a chain guard, 1966, $16.

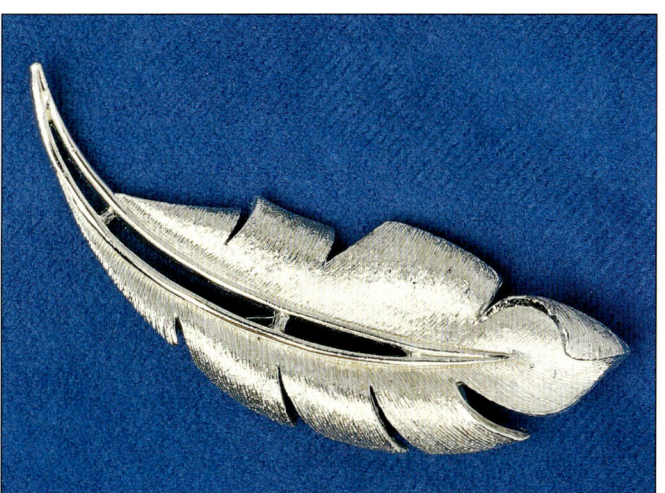

The edges are curled and the center split; is this brushed silver-tone pin a feather or a leaf? (3.5"). $21.

Large, brushed silver oak leaf pin. (3"). $21.

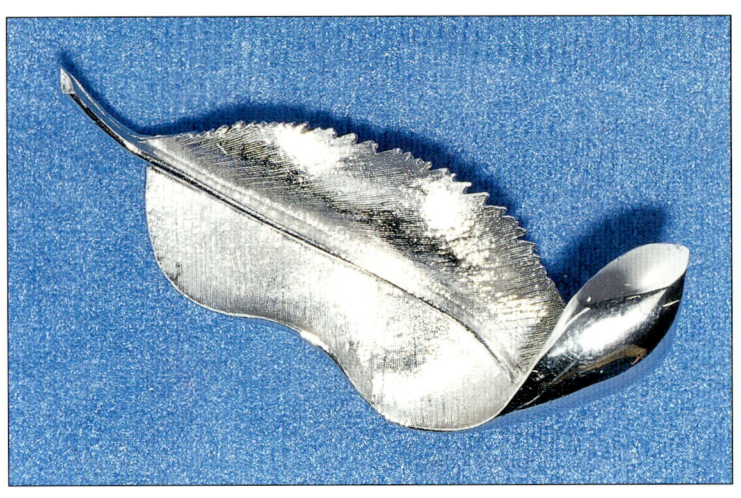

A curled leaf in a combination of brushed and polished silver. (2.5"). $17.

Lily Antigua. A silver-tone flower pin with four broad petals, its center done in high relief. Earrings not shown. 1969. (2.25" x 2"). $19.

Winsome. A charming silver pin/pendant with an embossed flower design. 1981. (1") *Courtesy of Dawn Levickas.* $18.

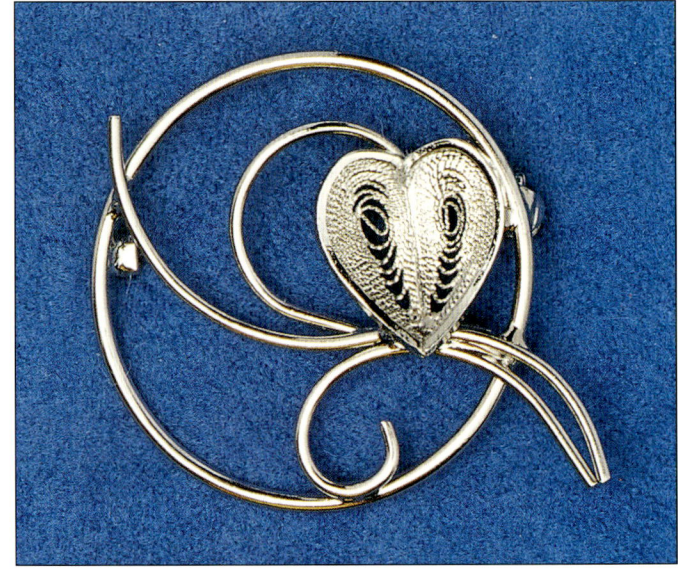

Delicate circle pin with what looks to be a butterfly with heart shaped filigree wings. (1.5" x 1.25"). $20.

This shiny pin looks like a silver dahlia just bursting into bloom. (3" x 2"). $21.

Love Knot. A silver-tone braid tied in a loose knot. Matching earrings not shown. For a later version in gold-tone, see p. 168. 1969. (1.5" x 1"). $16.

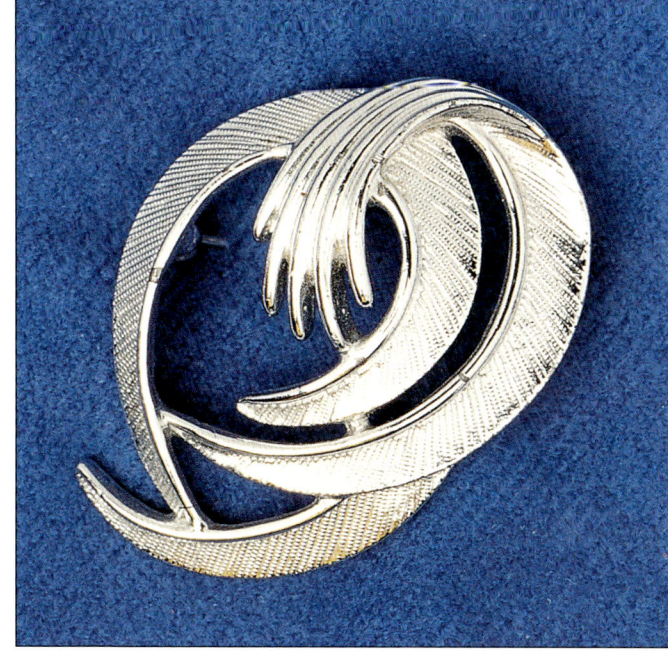

Curled feather in brushed and polished silver-tone. (1.5" x 1"). $18.

Snowflake. From the early 1970s, silver icicles are joined together to make a wreath of stylized snowflakes. This pin was offered only once, in the spring of 1973. Other pieces of the same name were sold in 1964 and 1968 (not shown). $24.

Starfish. Tiny silver beads and "barnacles" adorn this pin. The matching earrings and the gold-tone version are not shown. (Just under 2"). $24.

Tie 'n Tassel. The circle at the top of this stickpin is covered in silver chains whose ends are left to dangle back though the circle's center. A chain-covered ball, again with the ends of the chain left dangling, hangs from the other end. Earrings not shown. Gold version shown on p. 152. (2.25"). $18.

Dainty Butterfly. Filigree pin from the mid-1960s. (1" x 1.25"). $18.

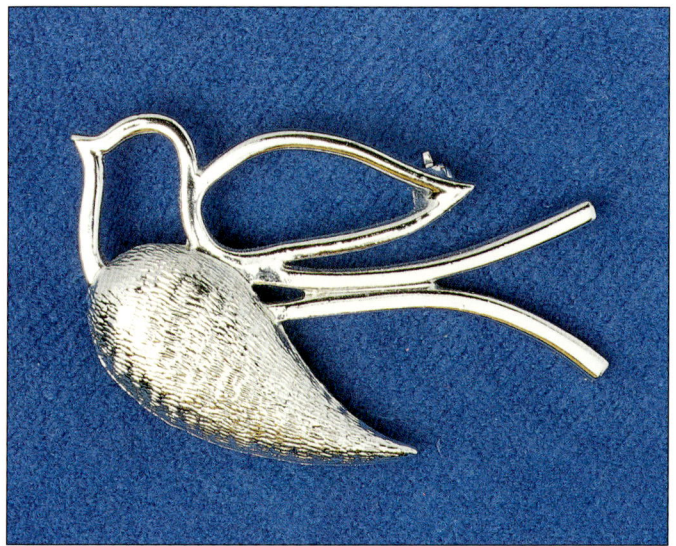

Songbird. From the early 1960s, a delightful silvery pin. (2" x 1.25"). $24.

Gracefully curving silver bands form this stylized, prancing pony. (1.75" x 1.25"). $24.

Pear Bright. A brushed silver pear. The gold pear is on p. 170. 1969. (2" x 1.5"). $24.

Helmsman. A very detailed figural tie clip with a helmsman in full wet-weather gear at a ship's wheel. 1965. (.75" x 1"). $18.

Gleaming Bows. The bows are made of silver-tone threads connected to seven gleaming beads in the center. Bracelet not shown. The full set of Gleaming Bows in gold-tone may be seen on p. 155. Mid-1960s. (1.5"). $12.

Multiplicity. Both textured and polished silver circles surround three slender leaves in the clips of this sweater guard. The connecting double chain with grooved silver links looks heavy but is actually quite lightweight. The removable clips are often described as earrings, but unless you want to pierce your ears, we don't recommend using them as such. There are sharp prongs on the clips designed to catch in fabric or leather. Mid-1960s. (Clips, 1.5" x 1"; Chain, 7"). $28.

These snowflake earrings are 1.5", and the lacy points are made of alternating smooth and etched silver-tone metal. We don't have either the 1964 or 1968 catalogs to determine if these are one of the versions of **Snowflake** mentioned earlier. $22.

Two pair of silver earrings. Left: **To & Fro**. Textured silver hangs from the ear clip on the backside of the earlobe, while polished silver hangs in the front. Perhaps a more appropriate name would have been "Fore and Aft!" They were introduced in 1969, and a pierced version was added in 1974. All were offered through 1979. Also came in gold-tone. (1.25"). Right: **Surfer**. Tiny surfboards, only .75" long, in polished silver (and in gold-tone [not shown]) were available from 1973 through 1975, with pierced versions added in 1974. $14, $12.

Classic. Delicately embossed hoop earrings, .25" wide. 1969. $16.

Tweedy is woven silver (1972), and **Yesterdays** (1976-77) is a rectangle with a polished center, possibly to engrave, surrounded by etched scrollwork. **Tweedy** also came in gold-tone (not shown). $16 ea.

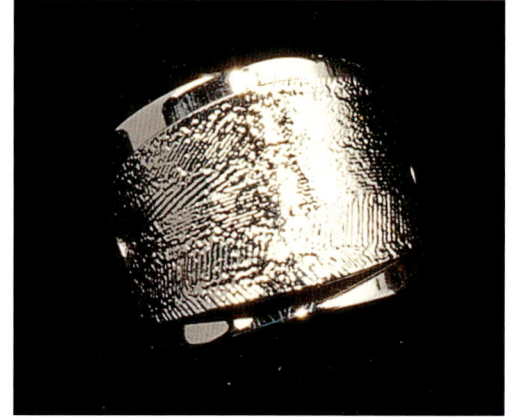

Sassy Hoops. Nearly .75" wide and 1" across, these are classic silver hoops that will never go out of style. 1975-79. $18.

Silvery Odyssey. Wide silver band with a brushed ribbon of silver fastened to the top. A full set of the Odyssey line is shown in gold on p. 155. $14.

Silver and Gold

The combination of gold and silver is very popular today, but rare in the world of Emmons. There are a few wonderful examples shown in the catalogs that we have not been able to find.

Polished gold melds into brushed silver-tone in the lazy loops of this necklace. Marked with an Emmons crown tag. Earrings not shown. (14.5"). $22.

We know this set is Emmons because of the "EmJ" mark on the back of one of the leaves. From a 1959 copyright description that reads, "Leaf motif; gold and silver necklace," we believe this is **Vogue**. (Necklace, 16"; Bracelet, 7"). $22, $12.

Ultima II. A two-piece necklace that can be worn together or separately. The loop of the silver-tone piece fits through the gold-tone filigree loop from the underside. The silver-tone chain is 18" and the loop 3" x 2.25"; the gold-tone chain is 15" and the loop 2.75" x 2.25". This was a Boutique Collection item from the mid-1970s. $22.

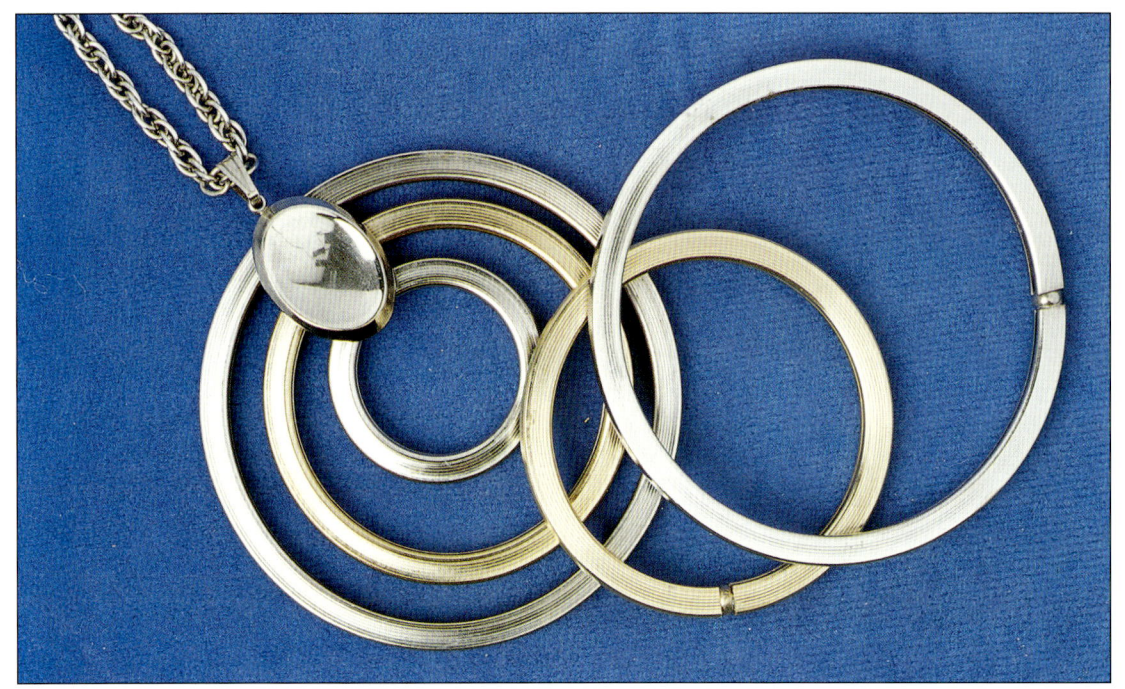

Fashion Bangles. "Take-Apart pendant. Large silvery bangle removable to wear as a bracelet. The golden bangle is removable for a child's bangle bracelet."— *Caroline Emmons Showcase Christmas 1974*. This was part of the first Boutique Collection. We are using a second set to illustrate the separated bangles. (Silvery Bangle, 3"; Golden Bangle, 2"). $23.

A pair of feathers in silver and gold. (Pin, 3.75"; Earrings, 1.75"). $24, $16.

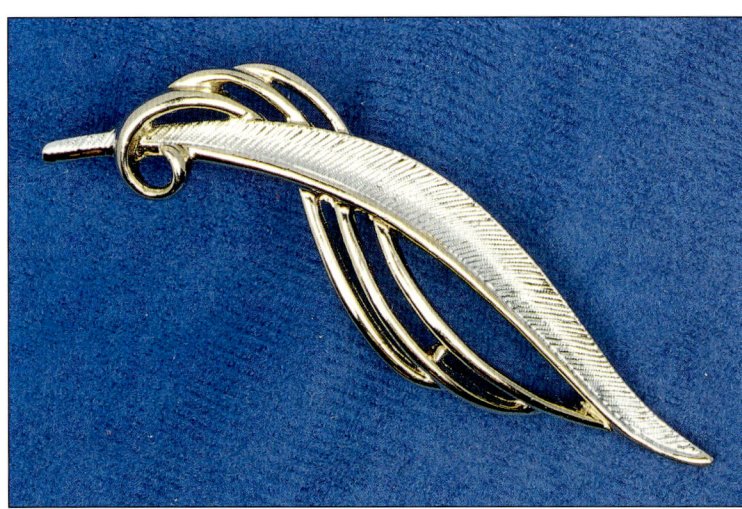

Brushed silver and polished gold catches the eye in this stylized feather. (3" x .75"). $19.

Just Gold

Every Emmons collection featured many gold-toned designs that ranged from the very simple to the incredibly ornate. Some designs consisted of just a single piece; others complete sets. As we noted in our introduction to the section on Just Silver, it wasn't until the 1970s that designs were commonly issued in both gold- and silver-tone. Thus, many of these pieces exist only in the gold-tone shown here.

Lovely older set with lots of detailing. Although the necklace is two-tone—the small teardrops and the "stirrup" in the pendant are silver—we believe the owner had something to do with that. The earrings are completely gold-tone. (Necklace, 18"; Earrings, 1.25"). $24, $16.

Fashion Flair. "Beauty and versatility abound in Emmons' newest special gift to Queen Hostesses. Satiny smooth strands of golden allure in an intricate design are enhanced by a polished slide bar which features its mobility and lends further prestige and distinction for the most elegant occasion. Adjustable bracelet and luscious drop Earrings complete its classic appointments. FASHION FLAIR is tailor-perfect for daytime wear, too—as graceful Sautoir with sweaters or dresses. And, with a touch of the finger, the drop earrings become smart button earrings. Your Fashion Show Director will be happy to show you all its fashion magic tricks. So much versatility…so exquisite an Ensemble—FASHION FLAIR will be desired by all who see it!"—*Emmons Showcase 1965*. (Necklace, each strand 12"; Bracelet, 8"; Earrings, 2"). $33, $20, $13.

Pirates Gold. Bright gold medallions stamped with a delicate floral design. Each medallion is .75" long. Mid-1950s. (Choker, 15"; Bracelet, 6.75"; Earrings, 1.25"). $19, $11, $7.

This heavy gold chain is tipped with openwork fobs in the shape of wax seals. When viewed straight on, the fobs on the lariat and bracelet have the look of a Jack O' Lantern! The faces are not evident in the smaller, more delicate fobs of the earrings. This set also came in silver-tone. (Lariat, 36"; Bracelet, 6"; Earrings, 1.5"). $30, $17, $12.

Tie 'n Tassel and **Sophisticate** (incomplete). Eight fine chains make up the necklace called **Sophisticate**, and they hold a removable pendant consisting of two gold, mesh-covered balls from which hangs a tassel. It came with a bracelet section (missing). The accompanying **Tie 'n Tassel** stick pin also makes use of gold mesh covering a wide circle shape at one end of the pin and a miniature of the pendant tassel on the other. Ten fine gold chains hang from earrings that were originally called **Sophisticate** and later called **Tie 'n Tassel**. Also came in silver-tone, p. 146. Early 1970s. (Necklace, 21"; Pendant, 3.5"; Stickpin, 2.25"; Earrings, 2"). $34, $18, $13.

The design on these burnished gold ovals, framed in dainty scrolls, looks as though it has been pierced into the metal. (Necklace, 13"; Bracelet, 7"; Earrings, 1"). $21, $13, $8.

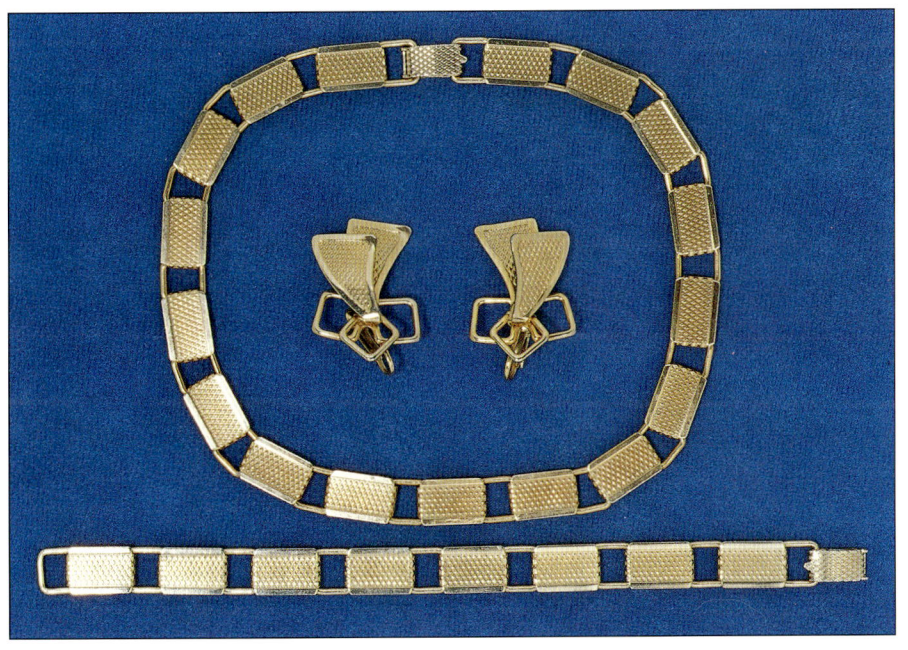

Rectangular textured-gold links make up this lightweight bracelet. The earrings are fashioned of the same textured gold but in more of a scarf shape threaded through squares of gold. (Necklace, 14"; Bracelet, 7"; Earrings, 1.25"). $18, $16, $12.

Is this set **Golden Braids**? We found a copyright listing of that name dated September 8, 1961, but there is no description. The different shapes and finishes do indeed give the illusion of braids. The set is quite heavy. (Necklace, 15"; Bracelet, 6.5"; Earrings, 1"). $23, $14, $9.

First Lady. "Textured swirling petals give you a golden Ensemble that will win a first place in your jewelry collection …"—*Emmons Showcase 1965.* (Necklace, 15"; Earrings, 1.25"). $18, $12.

This set is reversible. The pendants are brushed gold on one side and covered with tiny gold dots on the other. The scroll-work clasp on the earrings is the same on both sides, allowing the wearer to turn the earrings to match the necklace. (Necklace, 15"; Earrings, 2.25"). $21, $14.

Golden Blossom. This set was a selection for a Royal Princess Hostess. A bright gold flower with curly petals has a stem and leaves of brushed gold. The depth of the flower is .5". 1970-71. (Pin, 2.25"; Earrings, 1"). $18, $12.

Golden Blossom ring. (1"). $16.

A set marked "EmJ" of alternating brushed and polished gold leaves. When worn, the shiny leaves peek from behind the earlobe. 1950s. (Bracelet, 7"; Earrings, each leaf 1" x .75"). $16, $14.

Golden Odyssey (spelled "Odessey" in the mid-1970s). Ribbons of brushed gold appear to have been starched and attached to the outside of this bracelet, ring, and earrings. The large earrings are clips and the smaller pierced. (Bracelet, 2.5" dia.; Clip Earrings, 1" x .75"; Pierced Earrings, .75" x .5"). $18, $12, $12. Ring, $14.

Autumn Echoes. Brushed gold maple leaves with a thick center vein. Early 1960s. (Pin, 2.5" x 2.25"; Earrings, 1"). $21, $14.

Gleaming Bows. Bows made of shining threads with centers of highly polished gold balls. In the earrings, the bows are folded in the middle and clasped together to create a circular spray of bows. Silver earrings can be seen on p. 147. Mid-1960s. (Bracelet, 7"; Earrings, 1.5"). $18, $12.

155

Sugar Maple. This brushed gold maple leaf pin and earring set has polished gold veins and edges. Marked "EmJ." (Pin, 2"; Earrings, 1"). $18, $12.

Golden Fern. Outline of a fern in gold-tone. The silver set is pictured on p. 136. 1960s. (Pin, 3"; Earrings, 1"). $14, $11.

Instead of climbing the lattice, the ivy in this pin and earring set *is* the lattice! Bright gold-tone edging with brushed gold lattice filler. (Pin, 2" x 1.75"; Earrings, 1.5" x 1.25"). $18, $14.

Deep veins and detailed patterning give these gold leaves a lush look. This set is unmarked. 1950s. (Pin, 2.5" x 1.25"; Earrings, 1.75" x 1.25"). $21, $16.

Golden cup-like flower where brushed gold is overlaid on petals of polished gold. (Pin and earrings, 1.5"). $14, $21.

Are these gold-tone pieces with the twisted points and beaded edges stars? Or are they pinwheels? (Pin, 2.75" x 2.5"; Earrings, 1"). $24, $16.

Lily Fair. "The lily blooms so stately fair; In fashion jewelry for you to wear."—*Emmons Showcase 1965*. This satin-finished gold flower is outlined with crimped edges. (Pin, 3"; Earrings, 1.25"). $22, $15.

Gold Lace. Rounds of rippling, lacy gold-tone metal are topped with a faceted golden ball. Pin and earrings are the same size. (2"). $17, $23.

Button pin and earring set is brushed gold with shiny accents. (Pin, 1.5"; Earrings, .75"). $19, $14.

Concentric circles with grooved beads end in a flourish of golden ribbon. (Pin, 2"; Earrings, 1"). $18, $14.

Valencia. "The influence of Spanish art is envisioned in this lovely circle pin with scalloped edges and Florentine finish."—*Emmons Showcase 1966*. The pin in this set has apparently been the victim of harsh cleaning and no longer has a Florentine finish. However, the matching earrings still retain the black accents. (Pin, 2"; Earrings, 1"). $20, $14.

Each link of this substantial necklace and bracelet is .75" x .5". The chains are made of pale gold double links that close with toggle fasteners. (Necklace, 30"; Bracelet, 8"). $26, $18.

Bib 'N Bracelet. A triple strand of bold golden chains. The matching bracelet can be attached to make the necklace even longer. Also came in silver-tone. 1969. (Necklace, 24"; Bracelet, 7"). $22, $14.

Syncopation. Heavy pin/pendant in hammered gold-tone. Double ovals are adorned with six caged balls. Total length of pendant is 4". Early 1970s. $26.

Boutique Three. The plain chain (34"), the chain with the tassel (25"), and the chain with the locket (18") are all attached to a single necklace closure that keeps them tangle-free. All chains are easily removed from the closure and can be worn singly or in any combination. Both the locket and tassel are also removable. The silver version (not shown) was introduced in 1973. This set became part of the first Boutique Collection in 1974. It was in the line from 1972 until 1981. $37.

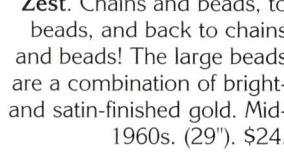

Zest. Chains and beads, to beads, and back to chains and beads! The large beads are a combination of bright- and satin-finished gold. Mid-1960s. (29"). $24.

C'est Belle. "A stunning Sautoir that personifies today's most popular features in fine fashion jewelry…the long, golden look; filigree accent for delicacy and delightful fringed tassel. Combined with fashion styling is its vast versatility as a bib, chatelaine, chain necklace, and pendant when used with pins and earrings. C'est Belle has its own delightful swing and sway earrings to match. In French, we say, "C'est belle!" In English—'It is beautiful!'"—*Emmons Showcase 1966*. (Chain, 25"; Tassel, 3.5"). $31.

Fashion Twist. At intervals along this 54" chain, you find golden love knots. Also came in silver-tone (not shown). 1978-79. $32.

Rope Trick. A heavy gold chain lariat has bright, brushed-gold fobs that are pierced at both the top and bottom. 1974. (Chain, 41"; Fobs, .75"). $26.

Starstruck (incomplete). Textured squares of gold are linked together to form a 19.5" necklace. It is shown with a 1.25" star charm (removable). There was also a 15" chain (missing) that could be added to make the necklace into a belt. Also came in silver-tone. 1976-77. $21, $8.

This choker is made of three rows of faceted rectangles. The outer rectangles are double-faceted; the center row is single-faceted. The original card shows the number 3649. (13.5"). $23.

Tiers of Lace. A fine, twisted gold chain is attached to a solid oblong shape that is attached to a solid cube. Five chains of various styles fall from the cubes to form a bib-style necklace. It is 20" long but can also be worn at 18". 1978-79. $24.

Viva. The box chain of this strikingly simple necklace is the color of rose gold and contrasts nicely with the yellow gold of the "V." It is from the Boutique Collection and was available from 1978-80. (17"). $22.

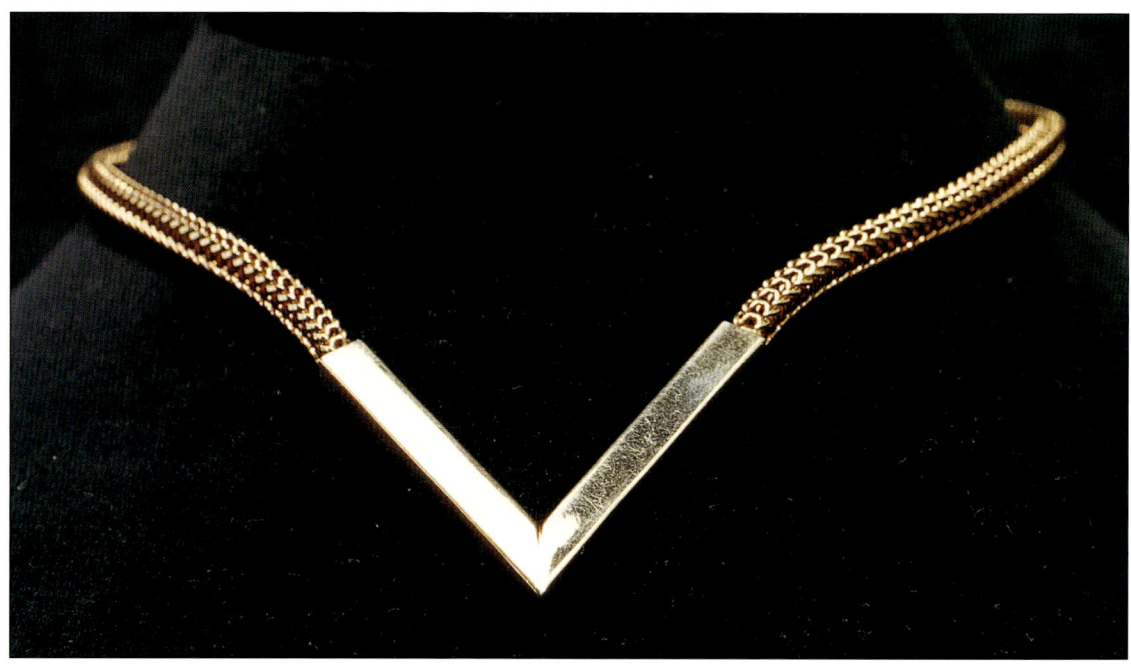

162

Collection of gold chains. Left to right: **Guys and Dolls,** a 19" barley corn chain (silver shown on p. 140), 1980-81; **Just for You,** "I", 16" long, 1978-80; 16" plain gold chain with an Emmons tag, but clasp ring with "Sarah 14k," 1979-81; **Starcast,** zodiac pendant in "Leo," 20" long, 1979-80; **Simply Elegant,** which came in 15", 19", 24", 30", and 36" lengths in both gold and silver, 1980; and **Just for You,** "A", 16" long, 1978-80. $18 ea.

More gold chains. Left to right: **Duet** (incomplete), dainty gold disk that was paired with a larger gold disk with a rhinestone center (not shown), 1975, $22; **Edith Ann,** a delicate gold bow (1.75") on a 16" chain, 1979-80, $18; a gold-filled heart (.5") on a 16" delicate chain from the Emmons Crown Collection, 1960s, $24; and **Sea Shell,** a brushed gold slide runs along a chain that can be worn at a 16" or 18" length, pierced earrings not shown, 1976, $16.

More gold chains. Left to right: **Rain Drop,** gold surrounded by silver; a Junior necklace (engraved with DL), 1978; **Everlasting,** also came in silver (p. 139), 1976; and **One and Only,** 1978. *Courtesy of Dawn Levickas.* $16 ea.

Traces. A large, open-work golden heart pendant. 1978-79. (Pendant, 2.5" x 1.75"; Chain, 22"). $21.

Medallion (incomplete). Part of a hostess set from the mid-1970s, this gold disk with filigree edging has "diamond cut" brush-like strokes in the center. The accompanying plain chain is missing. (2"). $21.

This handsome bracelet is made of heavy filigree shields in antiqued gold. (6.75" x 1.75"). $22.

Collection of bracelets. Left to right: **Quartet**, a set of four bangle bracelets, each with a different texture, joined together by a gold link. Silver-tone version shown on p. 142. 1969-76, $18; **Roundtowner**, an interesting hinged gold bangle, where the doubled wire bands fold over and into the loop at the other end, 1978, $21; and **Roundabout**, a hinged gold bracelet (silver version shown on p. 143), stamped with a fine basket weave design, where the ends curl back over the bracelet, matching earrings not shown, 1969-71, $16.

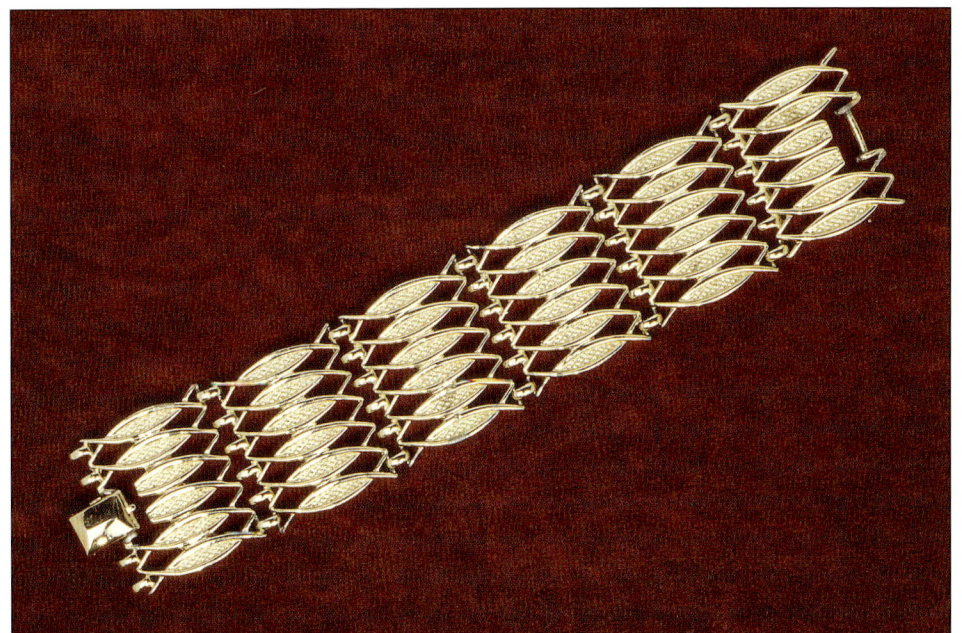

Wide (1.5") bracelet of linked fishes that are shiny gold, their bodies imprinted with scales. Pin and earrings not shown. (7"). $18.

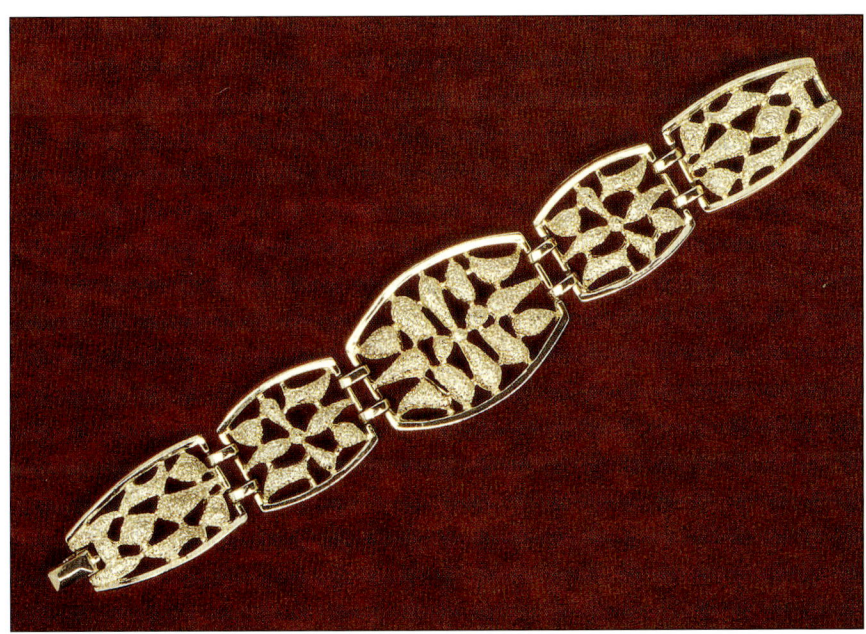

Frosty Lace. A bracelet of five, open-work sections in flocked gold-tone. The silver bracelet is shown on p. 141. 1972. (7"). $16.

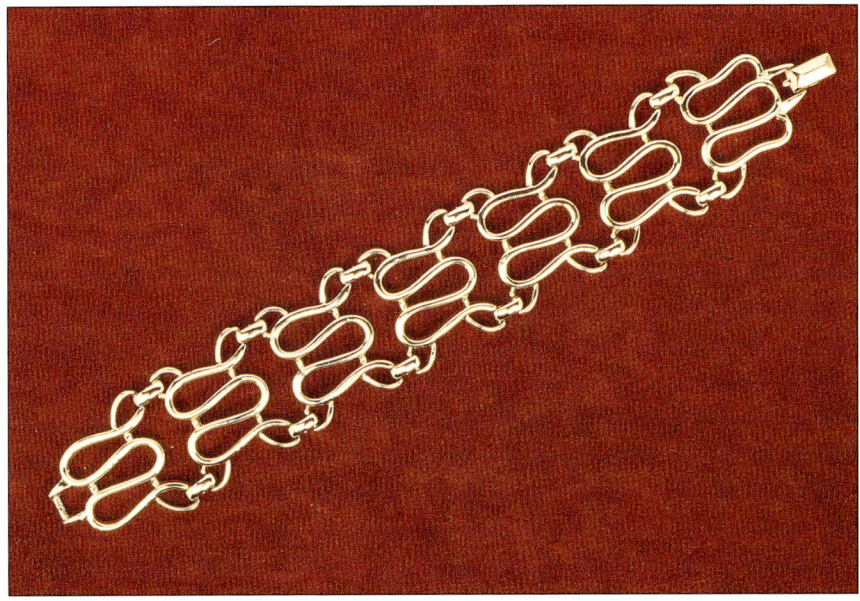

Cuff 'n Collar (incomplete). As though someone has done a loose crochet of golden wire, this bracelet came with an extender (missing) to turn it into a choker. The silver-tone version is shown on p. 141. 1971-73. (6.5"). $16.

Times Square. A gold mesh bracelet encased in solid, brushed gold rectangles. The gold version was introduced in 1974. Silver (pictured on p. 142) was added in 1975, and both were available until 1981. (6.75"). $16.

Five rows of golden rectangles form a very fluid bracelet. (6.5"). $17.

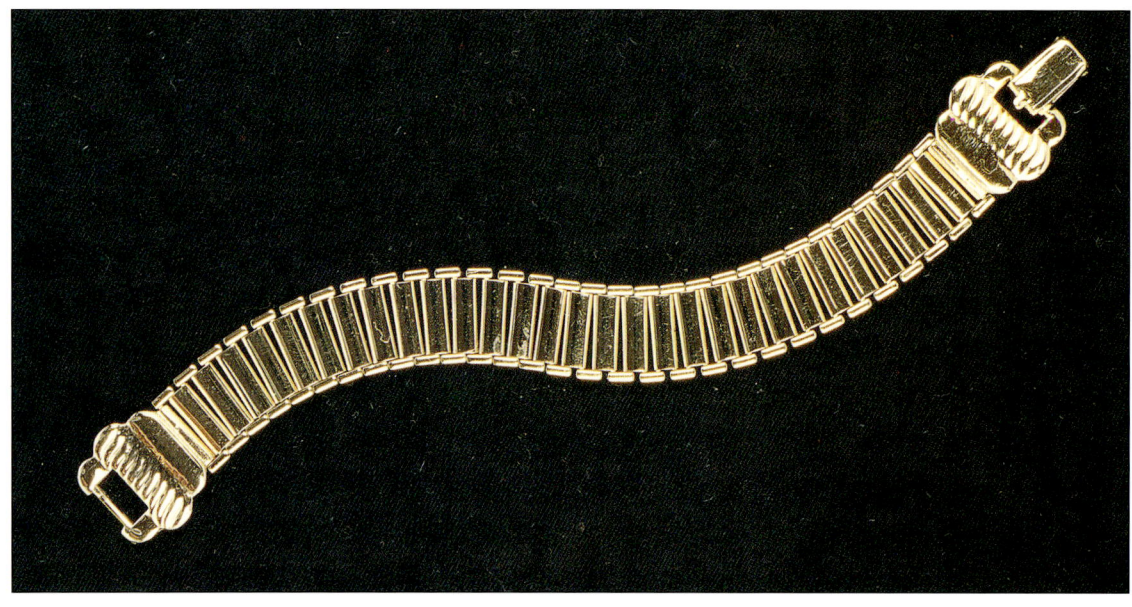

Palisades. Shiny gold rectangles are so tightly linked that this bracelet looks like a stretch watchband. Necklace and earrings not shown. 1950s. (6.5"). $14.

Whirligig. A single gold disk with raised ribbing in a swirl design hangs from a simple gold chain bracelet. Earrings not shown. 1950s. (Bracelet, 7"; Charm, 1"). $14. **Beehive**. A thick Byzantine gold chain with a heavy, yet small—just .5"—beehive charm attached. 1966. (6.5"). $16.

Charm Bracelet Chain. Part of the 1966 Emmons Crown Collection, this double link chain bracelet would be perfect for your collection of charms! Shown in its original box. It came in both sterling silver and 12 kt. gold-filled (shown). (6.5"). $21.

This hand-engraved, gold-filled charm was part of the Emmons Crown Collection. 1960s. (1"). $24.

Zodiac Charm. This Libra charm is part of Emmons' Crown Collection of semi-precious jewelry. It is hand-brocaded (meaning a raised design done by hand) on gold-plated sterling. 1960s. (.75"). $24.

This detachable fob with three charms, each on a 1.25" chain, came on an 8.25" matching chain with a filigree ball on one end. The fob has an Emmons tag. As there is no jump ring on the end of the chain, we don't know if it came this way originally or if someone made their own bracelet from another piece of jewelry. Fob only, $12.

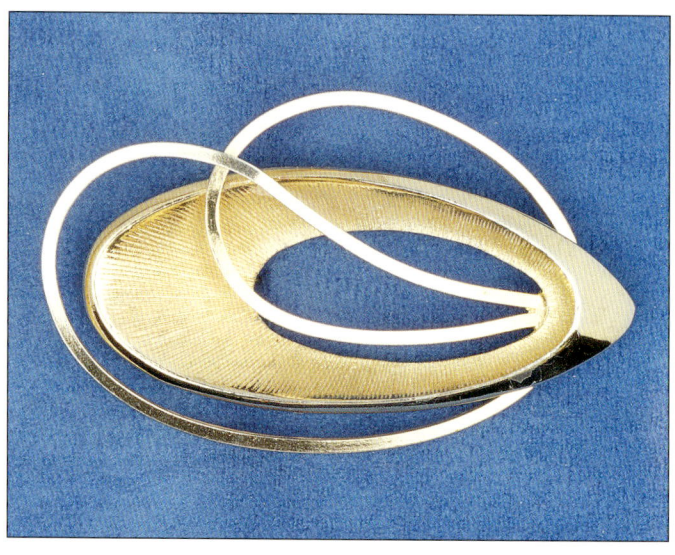

Orbit in Fashion. Pin of "…polished loops circling over the ribbed golden oval…"—*Emmons Showcase 1965*. (3" x 1.75"). $21.

This disk pin is decorated with etched circles topped by ivy-like swirls. The design is the same as that on the back of **Moonlight Pearl** earrings (see p. 48). (.75"). $16.

Golden Scroll. A domed, filigree disk is surrounded by a seven-point lace corona. Matching earrings not shown. 1972. (2"). $19.

Double-Take. A double circle pin where the shiny golden rings appear to be hammered flat in places. Also came in silver-tone. 1971. (Each circle, 1.25"). $17.

Love Knot. A series of knots in smooth and twisted gold-tone form a square. Pierced earrings were available from 1975-76. The pierced earrings and the matching ring (available from 1973-78) are not shown. An earlier version of **Love Knot** is shown on p. 145. $21.

A 3" bar pin with the look of a length of taffeta smocked in gold. $15.

Shown are two scepter-like stick pins in gold. The tops are round balls set in long prongs; the bottoms are filigreed baskets. (3"). $16 ea.

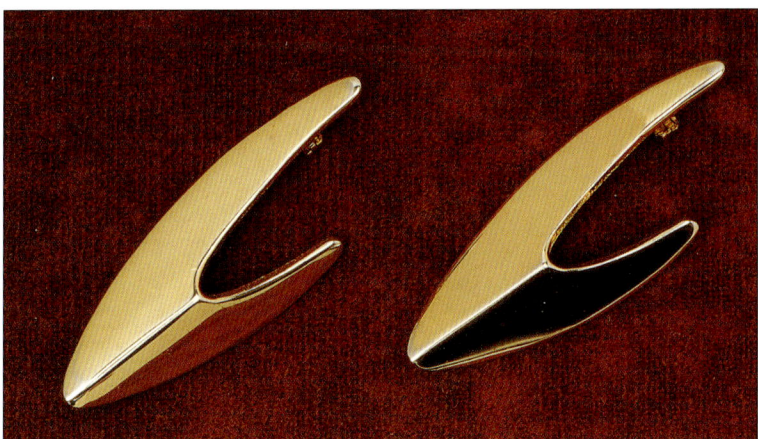

Pin Twins. "Trekkies" we are, and this sleek and simple pair of gold pins look almost like the uniform emblems from our favorite television program of the era. 1965. (1.5"). $26/pr.

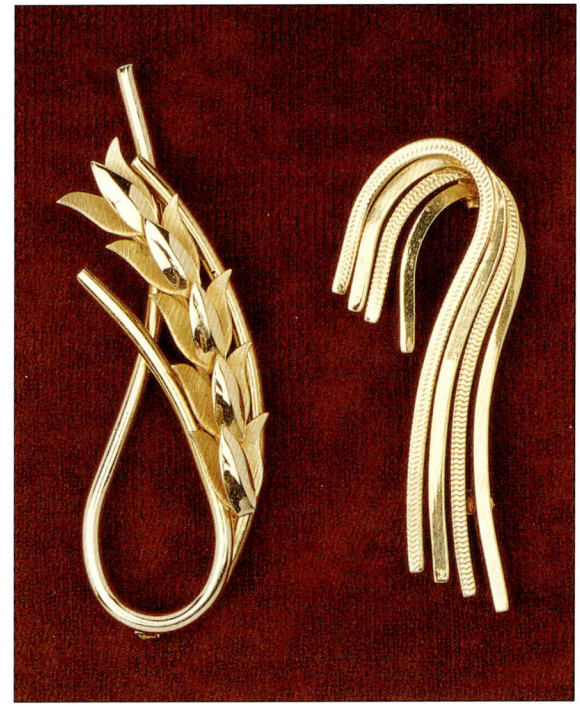

Left: **Golden Harvest**. A stalk of wheat curls back over itself. 1965. (2.75" x 1"). Right: Four gold bars, two etched and two polished, are set one on top of the other and bent to form graceful curves. 1950s. (2.5" x 1"). $18 ea.

169

A pair of baby birds in antiqued gold-tone with red rhinestone eyes sit on a twig chirping for their dinner. (2"). $24.

A golden angel fish, its eye and stripes are etched. (1"). $18.

A golden, ice-skating mouse with a clear rhinestone for an eye. We have heard his name is "Topo," but we cannot verify that. (1.5" x 1"). $24.

Daisy Time. "As welcome as the warm sunshine…"—*Emmons Showcase 1965*. The centers of these polished gold-tone daisies have been scored to give them the look of a real daisy. Mid-1960s. (1.5"). $21.

Pear Bright. Luscious, brushed-gold pear pin. The silver version is found on p. 146. 1966. (2" x 1.5"). $24.

Brushed and polished gold-tone metal flowers. (1.5"). $21.

Brushed-gold bamboo earrings. Bracelet not shown. (1.25" x 1"). $18.

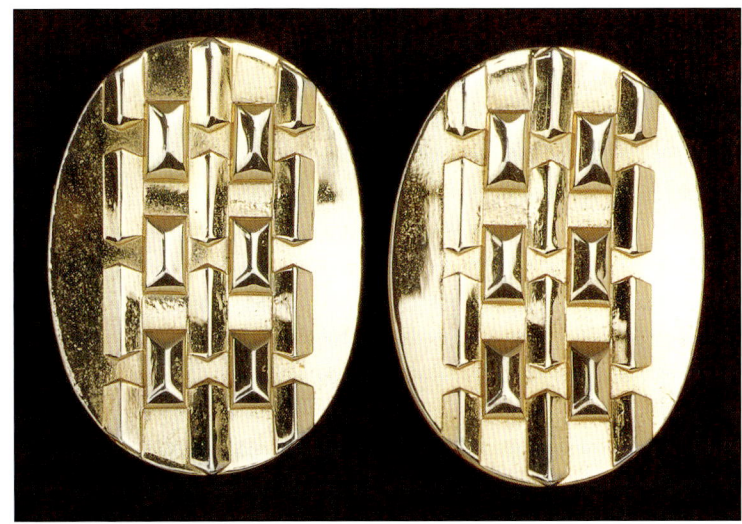

These earrings are curved golden ovals with a design of raised bars; dare we say tire tread? (1" x 1.25"). $21.

Zigzag. Overlapping chevrons in shiny gold-tone. Matching pin not shown. Also came in silver. 1971. (1"). $21.

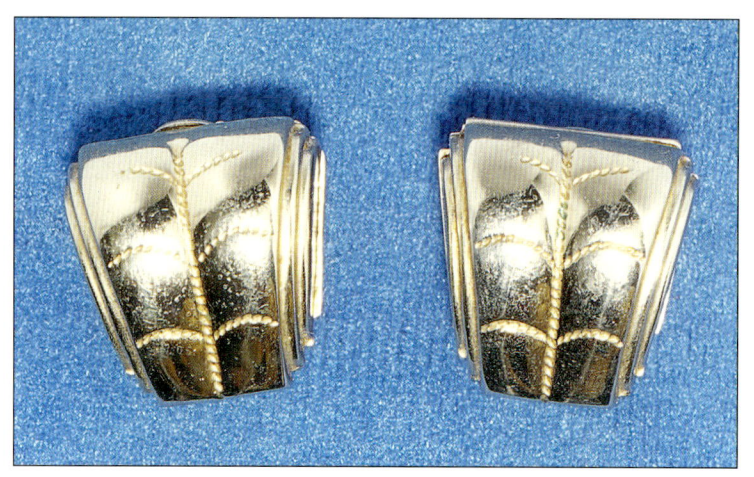

Etched, pillow-like gold-tone earrings are marked "EmJ." The matching choker and bracelet in silver-tone are shown on p. 134. (.75" x .5"). $18.

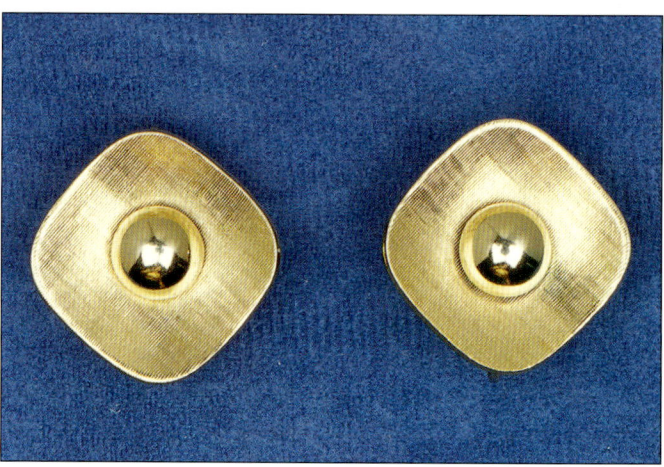

These earrings are slightly concave squares of satin-finished gold with a shiny gold bead in the center. (.75"). $21.

Adam's Delight. Or is it? One of these golden apple earrings is marked Sarah Coventry and the other Emmons. We can find documentation for this set in Sarah Coventry but the only connection we find to Emmons is the mark on the earring. (1.5"). $22.

Polished-gold stripes alternate with satin-finished stripes on 1.25" disks. The backs of these earrings and cufflinks are heavily embossed with a pattern of tiny circles and lines. These pieces are unmarked. Earrings hang 1.5". 1950s. $19, $19.

This elongated "X" is a barrette. Metal grooved toward the inside and polished on the outside edges. (3"). $18.

Signature. Gold scarf clip decorated with a round disk etched with a ribbon design, showing both front and back. Also came in silver-tone. Early 1970s. (Disk, 1"). $16.

Zodiac. Capricorn. 1975-78. $12.

An Unsolved Mystery

Despite extensive research and interviews with people who worked for Emmons at various times and at various levels of responsibility, we were unable to obtain any information related to the use of the pale blue cellophane-topped boxes containing the words "FASHION RIGHT BAZAAR from Harpers" on the side. The tops of the boxes contain the trademarked design logo (see page 24) that was registered in 1964. Some of the cards in the boxes contain the item's name and number, some only contain the number. Some have dates (1959 to 1961 on ours); some do not.

What's the mystery? Emmons did not advertise in the magazine *Harper's Bazaar* between January 1953 and March 1966. Nor is there a feature in this magazine named Fashion Right Bazaar. To what does "FASHION RIGHT BAZAAR from Harpers" refer?

If you know the answer, please contact us through the publisher.

The mysterious blue and white box labeled "FASHION RIGHT BAZAAR by Harpers."

Index

This index is limited to the jewelry designs pictured in this book for which we have been able to associate names. The few pieces of Sarah Coventry are so marked. Since with the exception of a very few rings all the pieces with a given name are either shown together or referenced in the captions, we have opted not to include type of piece in the index. If multiple versions of a design appear in the book, a date is given to distinguish between them.

Adam's Delight (Sarah Coventry), 172
African Queen, 120
Amber Cascade, 104
Amber Royal, 107
Americana, 127
Antigua, 122
Antique Star, 114
Antique Swirl, 122
Arabesque, 121
Arabian Nights, 138
Autumn Echoes, 155
Autumn Haze, 100
Avocado, 88
Aztec Lace, 84
Aztec Princess, 83
Beauty Points, 137
Beauty Vine, 46
Beehive, 167
Betsy Ross, 132
Bewitching, 58
Bib 'N Bracelet, 159
Black Magic, 59
Blooming Dogwood, 64
Blossom Time, 44, 52
Blu-Bud, 75
Blue Ice, 77
Blue Fire, 79
Blue Reverie, 84
Blue Rhapsody, 75
Blue Swirl with Tassels, 75
Bluebell, 78
Boutique Three, 160
Brocade, 134
Budding Romance, 114
Buttercup, 44
Butterscotch, 111
Calypso, 125
Camelot, 86
Candlelight, 126
Candyland, 19, 123
Candyland (Sarah Coventry), 19
Capriccio, 27
Caprice, 76

Caroline Birthstone Ring, 96
Cascade, 51
Cascade of Brilliance, 28
C'est Belle, 160
Charm Bracelet Chain, 167
Charmettes, 127
Cherries Jubilee, 93
Cinnabar, 94
City Lights, 36
Classic, 148
Classic Beauty, 41
Cleopatra, 116
Cloisonne Necklace, 126
Coco, 103
Colleen, 89
Confection, 66
Contessa (1965), 50
Contessa (1966), 50
Coquette, 72
Coralette, 114
Corsage, 39
Crimson Glory, 94
Crimson Rose, 95
Crown Jewel, 58
Crown Royale, 125
Crowning Glory, 81
Crystal Leaf, 33
Crystal Lights, 28
Crystal Spray, 34
Cuff 'n Collar (gold), 165
Cuff 'n Collar (silver), 141
Czarina, 30, 37
Dainty Butterfly, 146
Daisy Time, 170
Dawning Glory, 113
Dazzler, 62
Delft Romance, 82
Delicate Spiral, 138
Diamond Girl, 22
Dinner Hour, 36
Dolly Madison, 106
Double-Take, 168
Duchess, 87
Duet, 163

Edith Ann, 163
Embraceable, 143
Empress, 29
Endless Fashion, 138
Eternal Spring, 118
Evening Glamour, 62
Evening Glitter, 37, 62
Everlasting (gold), 163
Everlasting (silver), 139
Fancy Cat, 84
Fancy Free, 108
Fanfare (Sarah Coventry), 20
Fantasy Circles, 82
Fashion Bangles, 150
Fashion Crusader, 82
Fashion Favorites, 50
Fashion Flair, 151
Fashion Frost, 141
Fashion Tracery (black/silver), 58
Fashion Tracery (orange/burgundy), 110
Fashion Tracery (pink/gold), 96
Fashion Tracery (white/gold), 65
Fashion Twist, 161
Feminique, 99
Festival, 19, 74
Festival (Sarah Coventry), 19
Filigree Flower, 45
Fire Ice, 29
Fireworks, 32
First Lady, 154
Flair, 142
Flamenco, 61
Floral Antique, 116
Flutter, 111
For Him Cross, 139
Frosty Lace (gold), 165
Frosty Lace (silver), 141
Funflowers (green/yellow), 87

Funflowers (orange/yellow), 109
Funflowers (yellow/black), 109
Galaxy, 128
Garden Bouquet, 118
Garden Party, 81
Gay Capri, 63
Gay Marguerita, 86
Gibson Girl, 47
Gilded Wings, 108
Glamour Puss, 92
Gleaming Bows (gold), 155
Gleaming Bows (silver), 147
Gold Lace, 20, 157
Golden Blossom, 154
Golden Braids (?), 153
Golden Dynasty, 60
Golden Elegance, 22, 103
Golden Fern, 156
Golden Harvest, 169
Golden Odyssey, 155
Golden Scroll, 168
Golden Swirl, 95
Golden Triad, 30
Golden Veil, 57
Granada, 132
Grand Duchess, 53
Guys & Dolls (gold), 163
Guys & Dolls (silver), 140
Harem Girl, 99
Helmsman, 147
Her Elegance, 107
Hi-Fashion, 135
Honey Bunny, 71
Honeycomb, 108
Hootie (blue/silver), 84
Hootie (brown/gold), 108
Ice Bouquet, 34
Ice Queen, 37
Icicle, 36
Identity, 140
Illustra, 48

Indian Princess, 80
Indian Summer (beige), 108
Indian Summer (black), 61
Indian Summer (goldenrod), 112
Indian Summer (green), 90
Interlude, 51
Iridescent Rainbow, 67
Jade, 91
Jelly Bean, 91
Jet Cascade, 56
Jet Classic, 62
Jet Elegance, 22, 57
Jet Fantasy, 53
Jet Petite, 60
Jet Splendor, 54
Jeweled Charm, 130
Jeweled Dragonfly, 125
Just for You, 163
Kaleidoscope, 119
Lambie Pie, 60
Lavender Fair, 98
Leap Frog, 84
Legacy, 120
Lily Antigua, 144
Lily Fair, 157
Limelight, 90
Lite 'n Brite, 69
Little Something, 140
Lotus Flower, 96
Love Knot (1969), 145
Love Knot (1975), 168
Luster Leaf, 136
Magic Lantern, 65
Magic Wand, 94
Majestic, 27
Manhattan, 105
Mardi Gras, 124
Matchmaker, 50
Medallia, 122
Medallion, 164
Memories, 14
Mexicana, 80
Midas Touch, 70
Midnight Butterfly, 59
Midnight Lace, 131
Midnight Magic, 55
Milk 'n Honey, 101
Milky Way, 130
Mint Julep, 89
Misty Blue, 78
Mobility, 56
Moon Love, 141
Moon Mist, 85
Moon Shadows, 85

Moonbeams, 131
Moonglo, 121
Moonglow, 130
Moonlight Pearl, 48
Moppet, 91
Mother's Pin, 131
Mother's Ring, 37
Mr. Who-o, 84
Multiplicity, 147
My Favorite, 44
Mystique (1964), 61
Mystique (1975), 102
Nefertiti, 129
Northern Lights, 30, 37
Nostalgia, 119
Old Vienna, 108
One and Only, 163
Onyx and Lace, 60
Open Road, 142
Oracle, 90
Orbit in Fashion, 168
Palisades, 15, 166
Parfait Bib (pink), 97
Parfait Bib (yellow), 112
Parisian Delight, 101
Parisienne, 101
Pear Bright (gold), 170
Pear Bright (silver), 146
Pearl Glamour, 66
Pearly Buds, 43
Pearly Pinwheel, 41
Pearly Realm, 44
Pendulum, 56
Persian Treasure, 119
Pin Twins, 169
Pink Lady, 97
Pirates Gold, 152
Pretty Pastel, 123
Prima Donna, 52
Quartet (gold), 164
Quartet (silver), 142
Queen of Fashion, 10, 38
Queen of the Orient, 89
Raggedy Ann, 126
Rapture, 52
Rain Drop, 163
Rainbow Star, 20, 38
Raspberry Susan, 98
Reflection, 142
Regal Splendor, 114
Regalia, 122
Regency, 139
Renaissance, 81
Roman Holiday, 83
Rope Trick, 161
Rose Lace, 140

Roundabout (gold), 164
Roundabout (silver), 143
Roundtowner, 164
Royal Rose, 63
Salamander, 92
Sand Pebbles, 108
Sassy Hoops, 148
Saturn, 62
Scarecrow, 47
Scenario, 51
Scimitar, 121
Sculptura, 135
Sea Beauty, 58
Sea Flower, 42
Sea Shell, 163
Serene Beauty, 55
Serenity, 139
Shalimar, 85
Shimmering Lace, 31
Shining Faith, 139
Show Off, 139
Sienna, 102
Signature, 173
Silhouette (1961), 136
Silhouette (1969), 105
Silvery Fern (?), 136
Silvery Odyssey, 148
Simply Elegant, 163
Snow Queen, 72
Snowflake, 145
Snowflowers, 52
Soft Touch, 36
Songbird, 146
Sonnet, 135
Sophisticate, 152
Sorcery, 47
Southern Stars, 57
Sovereignty, 29
Spangle Dangle (white), 67
Sparklets, 15, 32
Sparkling Beauty, 30
Sparkling Burgundy, 98
Spectator, 135
Spellbinder (black/silver), 59
Spellbinder (white/gold), 74
Spirit of '76, 127
Sprig of Jade, 43
Spring Fever, 129
Springtime, 84
Starburst (c. 1960), 34
Starburst (1971, orange), 110
Starburst (1971, red/white/blue), 127

Starburst (1971, white), 72
Starcast, 163
Stardust, 33
Starfish, 145
Starlite, 40
Starry Night, 54
Starstruck, 161
Sugar Maple, 156
Surfer, 148
Sweetheart, 40
Symphonie, 53
Syncopation, 159
Tapestry, 132
Tie 'n Tassel (gold), 152
Tie 'n Tassel (silver), 146
Tiers of Lace, 162
Times Square (gold), 166
Times Square (silver), 142
Tin Lizzy, 35
To & Fro, 148
Today (Sarah Coventry), 139
Traces, 164
Tropicana, 67
Turnabout, 73
Tutti-Frutti, 112
Tuval Medallion, 95
Tweedy, 148
Twinkling Butterfly, 125
Two for Fashion, 45
Two of Hearts, 47
Ultima II, 149
Valencia (1965), 158
Valencia (1972), 99
Victoria, 88
Victorian, 98
Viva, 162
Vogue, 149
Waterlily, 42
Wavelength, 14
Wedgewood Cameo, 78
Whirligig, 167
White Camellia, 64
White Cap, 74
White Classic, 74, 132
White Olive, 46
Windmill, 41
Winsome, 144
Wood Chimes, 104
Woodland Charm, 107
Yesterdays, 148
Zest, 160
Zigzag, 171
Zodiac Ring, 173
Zodiac Charm (gold), 167
Zodiac Charm (silver), 143